# FREQUENTLY ASKED QUESTIONS ON THE DEAD SEA SCROLLS

# FREQUENTLY ASKED QUESTIONS ON THE DEAD SEA SCROLLS

Edited by

John M G Barclay

TRINITY ST MUNGO PRESS

*British Library Cataloguing-in-Publication Data*

A catalogue record for this book is available from the British Library

First published 1998 by Trinity St Mungo Press, Faculty of Divinity, University of Glasgow, Glasgow G12 8QQ, Scotland.

ISBN 0 9522311 4 X

# Contents

# PREFACE

This book has been jointly authored by members of the Department of Theology and Religious Studies in the Divinity Faculty of the University of Glasgow. Its origins lie in a very specific Glaswegian event of which we are immensely proud: the arrival in Glasgow (the only British venue) of the exhibit 'Scrolls from the Dead Sea' during the summer of 1998. We salute the skill of those who negotiated the staging of this exhibit in the Kelvingrove Art Gallery and Museum and are pleased to be making this contribution to its success.

The book is aimed at the general enquiring public - both those who have seen or will be fortunate enough to see the exhibition in Glasgow, and those whose interest in the topic arises for quite independent reasons. It is structured in the form of questions so that readers can dip in and out as they wish. All the questions are listed in the contents pages, and there are plenty of cross references within the text to lead the reader from one part to another. You may think of questions we have not answered here (or not asked in your form), but we hope to have covered most of the ground. There are suggestions for further reading at the end of the book which will lead you on into further and often more detailed treatments of these topics.

Unless otherwise stated, we have followed the translation of the scrolls by Geza Vermes. We would certainly encourage readers to acquire a copy of this or one of the other listed translations, as the best way to get the feel for what the scrolls represent is to read them for yourself and so let these 2000-year old texts spark off your own imagination and enquiry.

I am grateful for the help of a team of authors in this enterprise. Johanna Stiebert and Shiu-Lun Shum, research students in the Department, wrote most of Section Two between them. Of the staff, Joel Marcus wrote the bulk of Section Four and the first-person account of community-life in Section Three, while providing much-valued advice and support as the project developed. John Riches wrote Section Five, and Robert Carroll the final segment of Section Three; Alastair Hunter contributed to parts of Sections Two and Four and prepared the whole manuscript for publication. I own up to Section One, the first part of Section Three (with help from Johanna Stiebert) and the general editorial role. Finally, Jane Elliott, an undergraduate, read the whole manuscript with a fine eye for detail and made several important suggestions for its improvement. My thanks are due to all the above, who proved that collaborative work can be an enriching experience for all concerned.

While trying to provide straightforward answers to simple questions, there is always a danger of over-simplification. Since the chief goal of scholarship in our field is to ask good questions, which may not in fact be answerable, it goes against the grain to be answering them all the time, and without the space for qualification, nuance and hedging of bets! But we hope these answers will draw you in to ask further questions of your own and thus to develop your own journey of exploration into one of the most fascinating, tantalising and puzzling archaeological discoveries of all time.

John Barclay
March 1998

# ABBREVIATIONS

Qumran Texts          (for system of abbreviation, see pp.7-8)

| | |
|---|---|
| 1QapGen | The Genesis Apocryphon |
| 1QH | The Thanksgiving Scroll (The Thanksgiving Hymns) |
| 1QM | The War Scroll (The War Rule) |
| 1QpHab | Commentary on Habakkuk |
| 1QS | The Community Rule |
| 1QSa | The Rule of the Congregation (The Messianic Rule) |
| 1QSb | Blessings |
| 4QD | Cave 4 copy of CD (Damascus Document) |
| 4QEn | Enoch |
| 4QFlor | Florilegium |
| 4QMMT | Some Precepts of the Law |
| 4QpGen | Commentary on Genesis |
| 4QpIs | Commentary on Isaiah |
| 4QprNab | The Prayer of Nabonidus |
| 4QS | Cave 4 copy of 1QS |
| 4QTestim | Testimonia (or Messianic Anthology) |
| 11QMelch | The Heavenly Prince Melchizedek |
| 11QTemple | The Temple Scroll |
| CD | The Damascus Document |

Scrolls with a number and abbreviation of biblical book (e.g. 11QPs) are the version of that book found in the designated Qumran cave.

| | |
|---|---|
| BCE | Before the Common Era (equivalent to BC; see Chronology) |
| CE | Common Era (equivalent to AD) |
| MS | Manuscript |
| MT | Masoretic Text (see Glossary) |

# CHRONOLOGY

As is now common in both Jewish and Christian scholarship, we have used the terms **BCE** (Before the Common Era) and **CE** (Common Era) throughout, in place of the traditional BC and AD. Although the eras they designate are the same, the Christian assumptions built into the old labels (Before Christ, Anno Domini) are offensive to some and seem to jar especially with a discussion of Judaism in this period.

How to describe the Judaism in the centuries either side of the BCE/CE pivot remains a controversial issue among scholars. An old label, 'inter-testamental Judaism' is now generally discarded (it presupposes commitment to the New Testament). This book employs the term **Early Judaism**, which distinguishes 'Judaism' as a phenomenon emerging after the exile (in distinction from the religion of ancient Israel), while recognising this pre-rabbinic era (i.e. pre-200 CE) as an early form of the Jewish tradition. We also refer to **Second Temple Judaism** as a label for that period after the exile (586 BCE) up to the destruction of Herod's temple (70 CE), during which the second Temple in Jerusalem served as a focus for a multiplicity of variant forms of Judaism (some would say, Judaism*s*).

Some of the key dates for understanding the Dead Sea Scrolls and their environment are as follows.

## BCE

197       Judaea becomes a province of the Seleucid empire
          (successors to Alexander the Great, based in Syria)

175-164   Antiochus IV (Epiphanes), who encouraged the
          Hellenization of the Temple and the Jewish state

166       Maccabean uprising against this process of
          Hellenization, led by Judas Maccabee

161-143/2 Jonathan, son of Judas, leads the rebels to victory, and
          is appointed High Priest by the Seleucids (150)

140       Simon's titles as High Priest and Ethnarch confirmed
          as hereditary.  Founding of the Hasmonean (or
          Maccabean) dynasty, which passes to:

          John Hyrcanus I (135-104)

          Aristobulus I   (104-3)

          Alexander Jannaeus (103-76)

          Alexandra (76-67)

          Aristobulus II (67-63)

          Hyrcanus II (63-40)

          Antigonus (40-37; executed 30)

37-4      Herod the Great


## CE

6-41      Control of Judaea by Roman prefects

30?       Crucifixion of Jesus of Nazareth

44-66     Control of Judaea by Roman procurators

66-73     First Jewish Revolt:  destruction of Qumran in 68;
          destruction of Temple in 70;  fall of Masada in 73

132-135   Second Jewish Revolt (Bar-Cochba uprising)

# 1 BASIC INFORMATION

## What are the Dead Sea Scrolls?

'The Dead Sea Scrolls' is the commonly-used name of the documents discovered since 1947 on the north-west shore of the Dead Sea, in a number of caves around and north of Wadi Qumran (8 miles south of Jericho). Only some are actually 'scrolls', since a large number of the original leather or papyrus scrolls have decomposed, leaving only fragments of material.

Other documents have been discovered in the area around the Dead Sea, for instance in the mountain fortress on Masada (at the south end of the Dead Sea) and in caves at Murabba'at and Nahal Hever (near En-gedi, on the west shore). These provide dramatic evidence of Jewish life at the end of the first Jewish revolt (66 - 73 CE) and in the course of the second (132-135 CE). But they are not generally included in the category 'The Dead Sea Scrolls' and they will not be discussed here.

## When were the Dead Sea Scrolls discovered?

The story of the discovery of the first scrolls, in 1947, is extraordinary, and has been told in multiple versions. It appears that in the winter or spring of that year three Bedouin shepherds, of the Ta'amireh tribe, were tending their flocks when one of them tossed a stone into a cave opening and heard something shatter inside. Two days later, one of his companions, Muhammad edh-Dhib, squeezed into the cave and found ten jars. Most of these were empty, but one contained three scrolls, which turned out to be a copy of the biblical book of Isaiah, the Community Rule of the Qumran community and a commentary on the biblical prophecies of Habakkuk. Later, more than 70 fragments and four other scrolls were found in that cave (Cave 1): the Thanksgiving Scroll, the War Scroll, the Genesis Apocryphon and another partial copy of Isaiah (see further on each document, Section 2). Naturally it took some time for these scrolls to pass through various hands into the open and the reach of scholars - a process complicated by the fact that the British Mandate in Palestine finished in 1948, which saw the birth of the state of Israel. Of course, as soon as these discoveries were known to be ancient and valuable, the search was on for others.

## How many caves have yielded material and how much has been discovered?

In 1952 the Bedouin discovered another cave near the first (Cave 2), which contained fragments of 33 manuscripts. Archaeologists then conducted a systematic search of hundreds of caves in the vicinity and discovered Cave 3, containing fourteen manuscripts and the enigmatic Copper Scroll (see below, pp.27-28). In the summer of that same year, the Bedouin found Cave 4, very near to the building ruins at Qumran. It contained more than 15,000 fragmentary manuscripts, parts of about 575 original manuscripts which had been stored in the cave. The state of preservation was far worse than the scrolls found in Cave 1, but the range of material far wider. At the same time two other caves were found in the immediate vicinity, Cave 5 yielding fragments of about 25 manuscripts, and Cave 6 fragments of another 30 or so.

From 1953-55 there were extensive excavations at the Qumran site, during which some further local caves were explored. Cave 7 had 19 very small fragments, Cave 8 had only 5 fragments, Cave 9, only one papyrus fragment, and Cave 10 one piece of inscribed pottery. It was the Bedouin who again made the last really significant discovery, in 1956. This was Cave 11, of whose 21 texts some proved to be almost complete: these included the Temple Scroll and the book of Leviticus written in the palaeo-Hebrew (old-Hebrew) script.

Thus altogether 11 caves in the vicinity of Qumran have yielded written materials. Since 1956 there have been extremely thorough searches of the area, including the use of sonar resonancing to spot covered-over cavities. However, these have turned up no further materials to date. It is just possible that some are yet to be discovered, but the chances are now slim. Whether there are other scrolls which have been taken out of caves but hidden away elsewhere is anyone's guess.

The documents so far discovered and publicly available number some 11 scrolls written on leather, one embossed on copper and tens of thousands of fragments of papyrus and leather, parts of at least another 800 original documents. By any standards, this is a fantastic haul of ancient documents. The fact that they relate to a formative period in the history of Judaism and the very time and place where Christianity was born makes them of enormous historical and religious significance.

## How well preserved are the Dead Sea Scrolls?

This varies enormously, ranging from near complete leather scrolls, damaged only at their ends, to tiny fragments of leather or papyrus on which only one or two letters can be read. In general, the dryness of the region has been the salvation of the material, which would otherwise have decomposed entirely. Some of the best-preserved scrolls were found wrapped in linen and placed in jars, while most of the fragments were loose on the cave floor and thus far more exposed. Papyrus is an extremely fragile material when old, and many fragments disintegrate on the merest touch. The circumstances of their discovery (see above) no doubt led to the loss or damage of many, but even today in museum conditions it is difficult to preserve and handle this material.

The material found in scroll form was naturally subject to decay in the very effort to unroll it; in many cases the sheets were stuck together by the decomposing ink. The Copper Scroll obviously presented peculiar difficulties, and had to be carefully cut to reveal its contents. In the case of caves where multiple fragments were found (e.g. Cave 4), it is hard to know which fragments belong together, and elaborate efforts have to be made to piece the jigsaws together. In many cases, decay of the material or the ink has made the letters indecipherable to the naked eye. Fortunately, in some cases, the use of infrared light and, most recently, the techniques of multi-spectral imaging, have revealed letters and words which were previously illegible, and it is possible that technology will continue to alleviate such difficulties in the future.

**When were the Dead Sea Scrolls written (and how can we tell)?**

It is obviously crucial to date these scrolls in order to place them in their original historical context. There are four means by which that can be done:

1    Palaeography (study of ancient handwriting): In the ancient world, most documents were written by trained scribes, whose formation of letters followed contemporary conventions. Those conventions gradually evolved over time and thus it is possible to place documents relative to each other by putting them on this line of development. Such a procedure requires some fixed points (documents which can be securely dated by internal evidence), but that is now available both for documents in Greek and for those in Hebrew and Aramaic. By analysis of the handwriting of the Dead Sea Scrolls, the date of their writing (or copying) can thus be fixed with some degree of certainty. Scholars have distinguished three periods (the names of the latter two roughly corresponding to political conditions in Palestine):

archaic (250-150 BCE)

Hasmonean (150-30 BCE)

Herodian (30 BCE-68 CE)

Within these periods, some scholars would distinguish early and late periods, and thus offer dates for each document within a span of 25 or 30 years. Not everyone would accept that palaeography can be that accurate, but it is generally acknowledged as offering a secure 'ball-park' date, especially as other tests have mostly confirmed its conclusions on the date of the scrolls. Palaeography would date most of the scrolls to the Hasmonean and Herodian ages, with only a few from the 'archaic' period and none from after 68 CE (with the possible exception of the Copper Scroll). Of course, this analysis measures the date when the documents were copied, not the date when they were composed.

2    Accelerator Mass Spectrometry: Radio-carbon dating was first discovered about 50 years ago, but carbon-14 testing requires the destruction of too much material to be usable on the scrolls (it was used on some linen used to wrap a scroll and suggested the date 33 CE, plus or minus 200 years). In recent years the new Accelerator Mass Spectrometry technology has been developed, which requires much less material; in almost every case it has confirmed the dates reached by palaeography, though in one exception it placed a scroll about 200 years earlier.

3    Internal Allusions: Very few of the Dead Sea Scrolls refer explicitly to contemporary events, and when they do it is often in a coded form which is difficult to interpret. However, in a few cases there are clear references to political circumstances, such as individual Hasmonean rulers (140-30 BCE).

4    Associated Artefacts: The pottery found with the scrolls can be securely dated to the last centuries BCE and the first century CE (on the linen, see above). Moreover, this pottery is identical to that found at the site of Qumran, where the buildings and coin finds date the period of occupation from the second century BCE

to 68 CE (when the settlement was probably destroyed by the Romans).

Thus all these methods combine to enable a confident verdict on the date of the scrolls: though some date from an earlier period (third century BCE), most come from the period 200 BCE - 70 CE, with the bulk dating from the first century BCE. These dates help to prove that the community and its writings were an established part of the Jewish landscape well before Christianity was born.

## Where were the scrolls copied and why were they put in the caves?

There is nothing in the scrolls to indicate their place of origin, but the fact that so many of the caves are in the immediate vicinity of the site of a settlement at Qumran makes that the most likely source; caves 3 and 11 are the furthest away, just over 1 mile north. (A few documents must be dated before the settlement of the site, and were probably brought from elsewhere.) The connection between the pottery finds in the caves and at Qumran (e.g. the same shape and make of pot) renders the association practically certain, while the discovery of ink-wells at Qumran suggests that it was equipped for the necessary scribal activity. Although it has occasionally been suggested that the scrolls originate from Jerusalem, and represent a library hurriedly brought down in an emergency, there is no good reason to doubt the Qumran connection; only the Copper Scroll, with its references to treasure-troves, including temple vessels (see below, pp.27-28), gives some room for doubt on this score (see the fuller discussion of this issue below, pp.30-32).

Thus, the Dead Sea Scrolls represent the books written, copied and studied by the people who lived at Qumran (we will discuss later who these people were, pp.34-39). The fact that biblical documents are so numerous suggests their special concern to study the Scriptures. It is a little uncertain which of these documents represent their own production and which they had gathered from elsewhere (as a 'library'), but the fact that they were placed in the caves suggests that they were all treasured. Some of the caves showed signs of habitation, but most seemed to have been designed only for storage. It is possible that the mass of documents gathered in Cave 4, without proper wrapping, were placed there for safe-keeping in 68 CE, when Roman soldiers arrived to attack the Qumran settlement.

### What languages are the Dead Sea Scrolls written in?

The majority of the scrolls are written in Hebrew, the ancient and sacred language of the Jewish Scriptures. A small proportion are written in Aramaic (the 'everyday' language of the region) and a few in Greek (the 'international' language of the day). All the fragments in Cave 7 were in Greek. (For recommendations on English translations, see Further Reading, p.101.)

### What sort of material do the scrolls contain?

All the books of the Hebrew Scriptures (= the Protestant 'Old Testament') have been found among the scrolls, except for the books of Esther and Nehemiah; there are also some Aramaic and Greek translations of these Scriptures. Secondly, there are a number of works which were widely current among Jews of the time but did not end up in the canon of the Hebrew Scriptures, such as the book of Enoch, the book of Tobit and the Wisdom of Jesus ben Sira (or Ecclesiasticus). A third category are those works which appear to have been written by the people at Qumran or the movement they represented (in a few cases it is hard to tell if documents belong to this category or the second above). These include rules for community life, hymns and liturgies, calendrical calculations and interpretations of the laws or prophecies of the Scriptures. For further details see Section 2. There are no specifically Christian documents (see below, pp.85-86).

### What do the abbreviated titles of Dead Sea Scrolls mean (e.g. 4QpHos$^a$)?

The main documents created by the Qumran settlement have received standard abbreviations, which can be found listed above (p.xii). In general, the abbreviations follow standard rules:

- the number at the beginning is the number of the cave in which the scroll was found;

- the Q indicates it is a Qumran document (as opposed to a papyrus found elsewhere);

- the next letters are the title of the document, e.g. S (= Community Rule), CD (= Damascus Document). Lower case p followed by the abbreviation of a biblical book indicates a 'pesher' (commentary) on that book (so pHos = pesher on Hosea); lower case ap indicates 'Apocryphon'.

- a superscript letter (such as $^a$ in the example above) indicates the particular copy of the document; some documents exist in several copies, which are thus identified by superscripts.

In addition, each scroll or fragment has been issued with a number, and many in fact are known only by their number. Thus 3Q15 is the Copper Scroll, while 4QS$^d$/4Q258 indicates copy $^d$ of the Community Rule found in Cave 4, which is also known as number 258 from that Cave.

### Where are the Dead Sea Scrolls now kept?

Several scrolls have had an exciting history, hidden at various times in shoe-boxes and the like. They have also been caught up in the political turbulence of the region, especially those stored in the Palestine Archaeological Museum in East Jerusalem which was captured by Israeli forces in 1967. Nearly all the fragments are now in the 'Scrollery', the records room of that museum (now called the Rockefeller Museum), while the seven major scrolls of Cave 1 are now displayed in 'The Shrine of the Book', part of the Israel Museum in Jerusalem. Otherwise, there are only some fragments in the Bibliothèque Nationale in Paris, while the Copper Scroll and some fragments from Cave 1 are kept in Amman, Jordan.

**Why did it take so long to publish some of them?**

The major scrolls discovered in Cave 1 were published with exemplary speed, and most of the other material from the other caves has also been made freely available in published form. The one major and scandalous exception has been the mass of fragmentary material from Cave 4, which included a very large number of documents (see above). This was explicable at the early stages by the fact that the material was extremely difficult to clean, read and sort, many tiny fragments proving difficult to place. However, most of that work was done by 1960, when 511 documents had been identified. Unfortunately, the task of editing and publishing the material was entrusted to just seven scholars, most of whom had teaching duties elsewhere. These refused to allow others to see photographs of the fragments until they had themselves provided a full scholarly edition, with transcription, translation and full commentary. The difficulty of the material and their scholarly ambitions combined to make this an extraordinarily long process, to the extent that some of the team died before their work was finished and others have still not produced the goods.

In the 1980s the size of the team was increased, and now numbers about 60, but pressure grew intense for at least some access to the photographs of these fragments. A few libraries had copies of these photographs, and in November 1991 the Huntingdon Library in San Marino, California declared them available for any scholar to use. That finally opened the floodgates, and now all the fragments are available in photographic form (on microfiche and CD-Rom) and most have been translated.

## Was there a cover-up?

The delay in publishing so many fragments has naturally led to all kinds of conspiracy theories. In the 1960s one of the official team of editors, John Allegro, fell out with his fellow editors and suggested that there was a Catholic strangle-hold on the publication process. The team had been led from the start by Father Roland de Vaux, of the (Dominican) Ecole Biblique in Jerusalem, since that institution provided the early academic base for scrolls study. But the original 7-man team was by no means wholly Catholic (aside from Allegro, an agnostic, there were two Presbyterians and a Lutheran), and other scrolls were edited by a wide spectrum of scholars, including prominent Jewish academics. However, as frustration mounted over the publication of the Cave 4 fragments, a renewed conspiracy theory was bound to arise, and in 1991 M. Baigent and R. Leigh published their best-seller, *The Dead Sea Scrolls Deception: Why a Handful of Religious Scholars Conspired to Suppress the Revolutionary Contents of the Dead Sea Scrolls* (London: Jonathan Cape). This alleged that the Vatican had a particular role in preventing publication of texts which discredited Christianity.

Fortunately, within a few months of their book, full access to the photographs of the scrolls became available (see above) and it became clear that, even if the Vatican had had such power, it would have had no motive for the alleged suppression. The fragments further the impression already gained from the other scrolls that there are many parallels between the Qumran community and early Christianity, and that some early Christian claims about Jesus had their parallels in the beliefs and hopes of contemporary Jews. (For a particular alleged parallel in 4Q285 see below, p.25.) But that was no surprise to scholars, or to informed Christians, and it is hard to see what in this material could be claimed to undermine Christianity. The cover-up theory was a hallucination: scholarly over-work, tardiness and selfishness are quite enough to explain the nearly forty-year delay in letting the world see what the Bedouin found in Cave 4.

**Why are the Dead Sea Scrolls significant?**

Briefly, for the flood of light they shed on Judaism - fluid and internally divided - in the two hundred and fifty years before the first revolt (c200 BCE - 66 CE). They show us the state of the biblical texts these Jews studied, and provide a whole new tranch of contemporary Jewish documents relating to that Bible. They also give us full, first-hand and fascinating evidence about one special movement within early Judaism which we otherwise knew, if at all, only poorly and at second-hand. What is more, this group shared much in common with the Palestinian Jews who followed John the Baptist and Jesus, providing illuminating parallels to the Palestinian Jesus-movement in its first two generations. Here, hidden for nearly 2000 years, is a mass of evidence giving us insight into a seminal period in the history of Judaism and Christianity. The rest of this book is designed to explore the varied aspects of this significance.

# 2    THE CONTENTS OF THE SCROLLS

## Which books of the Bible have been found among the scrolls?

Even to put the question in this way is to encourage some confusion. To a Jew, the 'Bible' contains the books of the (Protestant) 'Old Testament' in Hebrew, and in a different order to that of the Christian Scriptures. The 'New Testament' is of course not part of that Bible.

The Qumran community was Jewish, their 'Bible' that of the Jews (although, as we shall see below, they held various other texts in the highest regard). There is therefore little likelihood - and as yet only one fragment of disputed evidence - that we will find anything from the New Testament amongst the Dead Sea Scrolls. The biblical evidence surveyed therefore relates to the Hebrew Scriptures.

Only two books have so far failed to turn up in the Scrolls - Nehemiah and Esther. There is no obvious explanation for this, beyond the simple observation that the omission is a result of blind chance. Perhaps the rather frivolous and playful festival of Purim, for which Esther is the foundation text, was not felt to be quite proper by the somewhat strait-laced Qumran community. An explanation which has been proposed for the other omission is that Ezra and Nehemiah were originally a single scroll. Since the former has been found amongst the scrolls, we may conclude that Nehemiah is also there by default.

The following table, based on information given in James C VanderKam, *The Dead Sea Scrolls Today* (SPCK, 1994) summarises the number of copies of each biblical book found, and lists the distribution of biblical manuscripts among the eleven caves.

| | | | | | |
|---|---|---|---|---|---|
| Genesis | 15 | Isaiah | 21 | Ruth | 4 |
| Exodus | 17 | Jeremiah | 6 | Lamentations | 4 |
| Leviticus | 13 | Ezekiel | 6 | Ecclesiastes | 4 |
| Numbers | 8 | Twelve Prophets | 8 | Esther | 0 |
| Deuteronomy | 29 | Psalms | 36 | Daniel | 8 |
| Joshua | 2 | Proverbs | 2 | Ezra | 1 |
| Judges | 3 | Job | 4 | Nehemiah | 0 |
| 1-2 Samuel | 4 | Song of Solomon | 4 | 1-2 Chronicles | 1 |
| 1-2 Kings | 3 | | | | |

| | | | | | |
|---|---|---|---|---|---|
| Cave 1 | 17 | Cave 5 | 7 | Cave 9 | 0 |
| Cave 2 | 18 | Cave 6 | 7 | Cave 10 | 0 |
| Cave 3 | 3 | Cave 7 | 1 | Cave 11 | 10 |
| Cave 4 | 137 | Cave 8 | 2 | | |

It would seem that the most popular were Psalms, Deuteronomy, Isaiah, Exodus, Genesis and Leviticus. The first three of these are also the books most frequently quoted by the New Testament. It is of course not surprising to find the books of the Torah (the five books of Moses: Genesis - Deuteronomy) amongst those most popular with a Jewish sect. The prominence of Psalms and Isaiah might relate to two well-known features of the community: its interest in an alternative liturgy and festival calendar on the one hand, and its messianic and eschatological expectations on the other. These are also features which might align the community with certain New Testament concerns, without identifying it in any way with Christianity.

## Are these texts the same as in our modern Bibles?

In many cases the Dead Sea texts are substantially the same as those of the standard Hebrew text which forms the basis of modern Bibles. Known as the *Masoretic Text* (MT), after the class of scribes who preserved the ancient traditions and added vowels and accents in the period between 600 and 900 CE, this standardised text was assumed to reflect long-standing tradition going back to late antiquity. It was therefore of considerable interest to discover a body of written materials from as early as the 2nd century BCE which endorsed this belief. One scholar (Emanuel Tov) who has carried out a survey of the Qumran texts, estimates that 40% of them are 'proto-Masoretic'.

However, other types of text are present, suggesting that there was a degree of fluidity at the time. For example, it has long been known that the Greek translation of the Hebrew Bible (known as the *Septuagint*) differs significantly at a number of points, some only minor, but some quite substantial. To illustrate the former, the Hebrew of Deuteronomy 32:8 refers to 'sons of Israel', whereas the Greek has 'angels of God'. The version of Deuteronomy found in Cave 4 (4QDeut[j]) reads 'sons of God'.

More significantly, the Greek version of Jeremiah is considerably shorter than MT - raising questions as to the editing process to which the book was subject. The Hebrew manuscript 4QJer[b] represents a short text of Jeremiah which may have formed the basis of the Septuagint edition. This places the editing process firmly within the Hebrew tradition. It seems that there were at least two very different forms of Jeremiah in circulation in Judaea as late as the first century BCE. This of course has important implications for study of the text and canon of the Hebrew Bible (see below, pp.57-60)

In general, however, both the range of biblical books present amongst the scrolls and the degree of match with the text underlying the modern Hebrew Bible provide a remarkably important witness to the developing biblical tradition in the period 200 BCE to 100 CE.

## What material has been found other than biblical texts?

### 1    Material 'Supplementary' to Biblical Literature

In addition to the biblical material at Qumran, there are a large number of documents which have a considerably more fluid relationship to what has subsequently become the biblical canon. This is probably because such a concept as 'canon' simply did not exist at the time when the Qumran material was produced (see below, pp. 58-60). Nevertheless, such 'supplementary' writing may yield some clues as to how texts which have since become normative might have been mediated and interpreted. Furthermore, they greatly enhance our appreciation of currents in Jewish thought in the historical period which was the seedbed for both rabbinic Judaism and Christianity.

Here are summaries of the contents of some of the most significant examples of this 'supplementary' material:

### The Temple Scroll (11QTemple)

This is the longest of the 'supplementary' texts (in fact the longest manuscript found at Qumran). The scroll, measuring over 8.5 metres and originally consisting of 66 columns, was discovered in Cave 11 in 1956. Its name derives from the fact that it is chiefly concerned with the Temple: its building and furnishings, the order of worship, sacrifices and purity regulations. Its legislative details bear strong similarities with the biblical books of Exodus, Leviticus and Deuteronomy, and it has sometimes been assumed that the Torah served as the textual basis for this scroll. Its distinctive features, meanwhile, have been attributed to the idiosyncrasies of the Qumran community's inclinations. An alternative explanation is that the writings which became canonical were, at the time when this scroll was produced, still undergoing expansion and modification.

The words of the Temple Scroll are placed in the mouth of God, presenting its message as divine revelation. The regulations, covering a wide range of matters from measurements of the Sanctuary to laws concerning idolatry and incestuous relationships, have strong parallels with Torah regulations. Particularly interesting, however, are the divergencies. Like the Damascus Document (see below), but unlike the Torah, the Temple Scroll prohibits royal polygamy, marital relations within the city of the Sanctuary and marriage between an uncle and his niece. In relation to this last, Leviticus 18:13 *does* prohibit sexual relations between an aunt and her nephew, but as there is no direct ruling on whether a niece may marry her uncle such a union is licit, according to Pharisaic and rabbinic Judaism. The Temple Scroll, by contrast, explicitly forbids it. Again, unlike the Torah but like the Nahum Commentary (see below), the Temple Scroll pronounces the death penalty of 'hanging' (probably crucifixion) for traitors. Other distinctive features occur in the description of the prospective Temple. This is a very ambitious project, with the design of the outer courts having little biblical precedent, leading some to suggest that this is an eschatological (endtime) Temple. Such differences from the canonical material have sometimes been labelled 'sectarian', but other 'sectarian' features prominent in some Qumran manuscripts, such as mention of the Teacher of Righteousness, the Wicked Priest and the Liar, are absent from the Temple Scroll, at least as far as we know it.

## Other Interpretations/Paraphrases of the Torah

Several other writings interpret or paraphrase the Torah. For instance, the **Genesis Commentary** (4QpGen[a]/4Q252) adapts the chronology of the biblical flood story (Genesis 6-8) to the distinctive solar calendar of the Qumran community. It also explains some difficult points, such as why Noah curses Canaan when it is Ham who acted disrespectfully towards him (Genesis 9). A further example is the **Genesis Apocryphon** (1QapGen), of which 22 columns, written in Aramaic, are extant. This retells the Genesis story, but with considerable expansions. It recounts, for instance, the miraculous birth of Noah (whose father believes him to have been conceived by a fallen angel), and a request for Methuselah to travel to paradise to obtain clarification of the matter from Enoch; there is also an expanded account of Abraham's journey to Egypt, his return to Canaan and war with the Mesopotamian kings. It has been called a mixture between a Targum (Aramaic paraphrase of the Hebrew Bible) and a Midrash (commentary, often incorporating non-literal and legendary illustration, in order to answer questions arising from a biblical text).

As with the Genesis Commentary, portions of the Genesis Apocryphon may be apologetic or explanatory. In Genesis 12:15-16, for example, Pharaoh takes Sarah, Abraham's wife, and gives Abraham animals and servants, as if a deal has been struck between them. Perhaps because this implication was objectionable, the account in the Genesis Apocryphon stresses Abraham's grief and fear, while his acquisition of material compensation is delayed. Other elaborations are not apologetic, such as the literary flourish describing Sarah's physical charms. This is the only example of a *wasf* (a praise of beauty from head to foot) in Jewish literature, apart from those in the Song of Songs. Another matter of interest in this text is the account of Abraham laying on hands to heal Pharaoh - the earliest recorded instance of such a ritual in a Jewish source (it is later attested in the New Testament, e.g. Luke 4:40). In this connection we may also note the **Prayer of Nabonidus** (4QprNab/4Q242). Not unlike the book of Daniel, where Nebuchadnezzar is healed after a seven-year illness, this fragment recounts how Nabonidus, the last king of Babylon, is cured from an ulcer which had plagued him for seven years. But whereas Nebuchadnezzar was healed after acknowledging God's sovereignty (Daniel 4), Nabonidus is healed by a Jewish exorcist, who also pardons his sins. It is not stated whether this act of pardoning entailed the laying on of hands.

Other Qumran texts relate to the book of Genesis, though they are less well preserved. Among them are the **Flood Apocryphon** (4Q370), the **Joseph Apocryphon** (4Q372), the **Moses Apocryphon** (4Q375) and the **Testaments of Levi** (4Q541), **Naphtali** (4Q215), **Qahat** (4Q542) and **Amran** (4QAmran/543-548). These Testaments (all in Aramaic, except the Hebrew Testament of Naphtali) are poorly preserved but represent a well-known type of literature, the death-bed speech. The Testament of Qahat was the one exception where Accelerator Mass Spectrometry dating was nearly 200 years earlier than palaeographic deduction (see above p.5; the former suggested a date 388-353 BCE). The two columns which survive contain the instructions of Qahat (Moses' grandfather) to his descendants, urging them to lead pure and righteous lives. The Testament of Amran contains a fascinating vision of quarrelling angels, among them the chief angel of darkness, Melkiresha', who is also mentioned in another Qumran text, the **Curses of Melkiresha'** (4QTohorotD$^b$/4Q280). The name means 'my king is wickedness' and possibly pertains to Satan. The chief of light, meanwhile, appears to be Melkizedek, meaning 'my king is justice'. Melkizedek is the name of a priest-king in Genesis 14, also mentioned in the Genesis Apocryphon. Elsewhere, in **The Heavenly Prince Melkizedek** (11QMelch/11Q13), this name refers to an angelic being, cast as head of 'the sons of heaven', who presides on the Day of Judgment

### Pesharim (Commentaries)

These are another group of documents elucidating writings which entered the biblical canon. The word 'pesher' (singular) is a loan word from Aramaic and means 'solution' or 'interpretation'. The pesharim of the prophets Isaiah, Hosea, Micah, Nahum and Habakkuk all cite passage from a version of the relevant prophetic text and then supply an interpretation. Frequently this interpretation appears to concern contemporary events and sometimes cryptograms are employed. The enemies identified are the kings of Yavan (Greece) and the Kittim (probably the Romans). The **Nahum Commentary** (4Q169) names two

Seleucid kings, Antiochus and Demetrius, but in other cases the interpretations are more oblique. A 'young lion' is mentioned in the **Hosea** (4Q166-167) and **Nahum** commentaries, designated 'the last priest' in the former and described as 'hanging people alive' (possibly crucifying them) in the latter. This may be Alexander Jannaeus, a Hasmonean priestly ruler of Palestine (103-76 BCE), who is elsewhere recorded as crucifying 800 Pharisees.

Such interpretative activity might imply that the community who created it regarded prophetic literature as containing a message not only for the audience of its own day but also for that of a later time. The **Habakkuk** commentary (1QpHab) in particular appears to be designed for an endtime context, with mention of a 'final generation' and 'Day of Judgment', preceded by a time of turbulence and persecution. The prominent enemies are again the Kittim. Statements such as Habakkuk 1:13b ('O traitors, why do you stare and stay silent when the wicked swallows up one more righteous than he?') are interpreted with a particular, possibly contemporary, event in mind:

' ... this concerns the House of Absalom and the members of its council who were silent at the time of the chastisement of the Teacher of Righteousness and gave him no help against the Liar who flouted the Law ...'

There has been much speculation concerning the identities of the Teacher and the Liar. They are mentioned in many other places, including the only pesher on the Writings (the third division of the Hebrew Bible), namely the **Commentary on Psalms** (4Q171 and 173).

A further text resembling the pesharim, in that it cites and then interprets scriptural passages, is the **Midrash on the Last Days** or **Florilegium** (4Q174). This text contains echoes of 2 Samuel, Exodus, Amos, Isaiah, Ezekiel, Daniel and the Psalms, which are interpreted as yielding clues about the coming of the 'Branch of David' and 'Interpreter of the Law', either or both of whom may be messianic figures (see below, pp.74-76).

### Enoch

One important non-biblical text on which the discoveries of Qumran have shed much light is the book of Enoch. According to Genesis 5:24, Enoch was taken by God. Perhaps as a result of this unusual fate, he features prominently in Jewish literature of this period, where he is depicted as semi-supernatural, all-wise and granted to know the secrets of the universe. The fullest portrait of this figure emerges in 1 Enoch, a composite document preserved only in Old Ethiopic. Peculiar turns of phrase had long led scholars to believe that 1 Enoch was originally composed in Aramaic, and fragments of an Aramaic text of **Enoch** (4QEn/4Q201) were indeed discovered at Qumran.

Aside from Enoch, portions of texts echoing books in the 'Apocrypha' (Jewish texts included in the Septuagint but not in the Hebrew Bible) have also been found at Qumran, namely of Tobit and the Wisdom of Jesus ben Sira.

## 2   The Rules, Hymns and Hopes of the Community

### The Community Rule (1QS)

The Community Rule (also called 'The Manual of Discipline' by early scrolls scholars) is one of the seven documents discovered in Cave 1 in 1947; fragments were also found in two other caves (ten copies in Cave 4 and one from Cave 5) in subsequent years. The large number of copies of this document suggests its importance to the sectarians. It was originally attached, in the same scroll, to two other documents, The Rule of the Congregation (1QSa, see below) and 1QSb (a collection of blessings); however, the relation between these three documents is unclear. The Community Rule consists of eleven well-preserved columns. It has been suggested recently that it underwent a long process of redaction (editing and updating) over a period of time, by different hands. On palaeographic grounds, 1QS can be dated to the last quarter of the first century BCE, but one copy found in Cave 4 (4QS$^a$) is probably to be dated 100 years earlier, suggesting that it was originally composed in the latter half of the second century BCE.

The Community Rule contains a series of rules and regulations governing the life of the sectarians, a tractate on the spirits of truth and falsehood and a concluding hymn of praise to God. Scriptural citations and allusions are to be found throughout. The tractate on the spirits of truth and falsehood reflects the community's deterministic beliefs, and its sharp light-darkness antithesis is paralleled in the New Testament (e.g. John's gospel and Paul in 2 Corinthians 6; see below pp.63-64 and 94-96).

**4Q Rule of the Community[d] (4Q258/4QS[d])** is the longest and best-preserved copy of this document found in Cave 4 (on display in the exhibit). This manuscript can be reconstructed from two main fragments, fragment 1 containing the upper half of three columns and fragment 2 having the top half of five columns. Its script is formal, early Herodian, suggesting a date in the last three decades of the first century BCE. Due to an unusually wide margin at the right-hand side of column 1 in fragment 1, and the absence of any sign of stitching there, it seems most likely that the text of this copy of the Rule began at this point, which corresponds to the start of 1QS 5. Thus this copy omits the tractate on the spirits of truth and falsehood and focuses on the regulations for community life.

### The Rule of the Congregation (1QSa/1Q28a)

This short but important work, sometimes called 'The Messianic Rule', was found on the same scroll as 1QS. Its script shows that it was copied in the last quarter of the first century BCE. The work illustrates the eschatology of the Qumran community and its messianic expectations. Here regulations are formulated for the preparation of the last battle against the nations, in which all Israel will join in the Last Days; there is also a description of the messianic banquet which will be led by the Priestly Messiah as well as the Messiah of Israel (see below, pp.74-75).

One intriguing issue is the reading of a phrase in column 2, lines 11-12. There are two possible readings of this phrase: a) 'when [God] leads/sends forth (*ywlyk*) the Messiah'; and b) 'when [God] gives birth to (*ywlyd*) the Messiah.' In both cases the text concerns the origin of the Messiah, but if the second is accepted a special father-son relationship is implied between God and the Messiah. This would have a tremendous impact on our understanding of the messianic expectations at Qumran in particular and of early Jewish messianic beliefs in general.

### The Damascus Document (CD)

This work was first accidentally brought to light by a Cambridge professor (Solomon Schechter) in a genizah (store-room) of an old synagogue in Cairo almost a century ago. Due to the repeated occurrence of the term 'Damascus' and the prominence of the theme of 'covenant', the work was named 'The Cairo Damascus Covenant/ Document'. Its frequent reference to 'the sons of Zadok' also caused it to acquire another name, 'The Zadokite Fragments/Document'.

The manuscripts of this work found in the Cairo genizah can be distinguished, on the basis of handwriting, into Manuscript A and Manuscript B; the former (16 columns) can be dated to the tenth century CE and the latter (2 columns) to the twelfth century CE. These represent two different versions of the original composition. As to its content, the document had two sections: the Exhortations (MS A, columns 1-8 + MS B, columns 19-20) and the Statutes (MS A, columns 9-16). It is very likely that the Exhortation section served as the preamble to the Statutes.

Before the discovery of the Dead Sea Scrolls scholars debated the origin and date of composition of this work. Now the Qumran discoveries have led almost all scholars to the consensus that the document found in the Cairo Genizah should be grouped with those found in the Dead Sea caves, as belonging to one and the same Jewish movement. This consensus is built on both internal and external evidence. Internally, a comparison of The Damascus Document with the Dead Sea Scrolls reveals many affinities, both in terminology and in ideas. Terminological affinities include the use of the labels 'the Teacher of Righteousness', 'the Spouter of Lies', 'the Book of Hagi' and 'the Messiah of Israel and Aaron'. Common ideas include the dualistic struggle, the metaphor of the sect as an eschatological 'planting', and the notion of the covenant. Moreover, as external evidence, some of the material found in Caves 4, 5 and 6 has been successfully identified as fragments of the different versions of this document. These fragments not only support the consensus, but also help scholars to date the original composition of the Damascus Document. A fragment from Cave 4 can be dated to 100-75 BCE on the basis of its Hasmonean script, so the text is as least as old as that.

The Damascus Document offers information which helps us understand better the movement represented by the scrolls. The repeated reference to life 'in the camps' suggests that some of the members of the movement were not settled at Qumran but lived elsewhere, probably in the towns and villages of Palestine (see below, Section 3). These were allowed to have wives and children (CD 7:6-7; 19:2-5) and even to have contact with 'outsiders'. However, the document also gives scholars some puzzling problems, such as the reference to migration into the land of 'Damascus' (e.g. CD 6:5; 7:19). Whether or not 'the land of Damascus' should be taken literally remains a bone of contention.

**4Q Damascus Document$^f$ (4Q271/4QD$^f$)** is one of the eight CD manuscripts found in Cave 4 (on display in the exhibit). The early Herodian handwriting suggests that this CD copy was produced in the late first century BCE. Three fragments of this copy have been found, comprising 5 columns in all. The first column of fragment 1 (on display) represents unparalleled material, unknown from the Cairo genizah versions of CD, applying the law of selling and buying land (Leviticus 15:14) to the arrangement of marriages; this gives important insight into the sectarian interpretation of the law. In the second column of this fragment there are regulations on tithing and on separation from impure things (especially those used for pagan worship).

Fragments 2 and 3 of this manuscript give, respectively, various rules about oaths and a series of prohibitions.


### The War Scroll (1QM)

This is one of the seven scrolls found in Cave 1 in 1947. Later, several fragmentary copies were found in Cave 4 and these give a little help to scholars reconstructing the text of this document, while also presenting some variant readings. The formal early Herodian script of 1QM suggests that this copy was produced in the final decades of the first century BCE, while the oldest Cave 4 manuscript (4Q493) dates from 100-50 BCE and shows that its original composition was at least that old.

Like the Rule of the Congregation, the War Scroll envisages the final, cosmic battle against the nations and against those unfaithful to the covenant, all described as 'the sons of Darkness.' This is the war that will end all wars and bring about final peace on earth. It is cosmic, not because it is a 'Star Wars' battle, but one which involves both human and angelic beings. The sect was convinced that the ultimate victory in the battle between 'the sons of the Light' and 'the sons of Darkness' belongs to God alone (1QM 11:1-12). It is God's intervention which ends the battle and brings final triumph for His people.

The document is composed of three main types of material: rules and tactics for the preparation of the battle; hymn-like prayers for victory; and details of the engagements of the War. It seems to have been intended to offer its readers hope that all their afflictions were part of God's plan and that they would finally be vindicated by God. The document implies that the sect was a political as well as a religious community.

Readers familiar with the Book of Revelation in the New Testament will find in 1QM such parallels as common use of the 'holy war' traditions and expectations of the victory of God and His faithful elect in a final cosmic battle between good and evil. The notion that God's faithful people must suffer in the endtime also occurs in the New Testament, for instance in Mark 13.

**4Q285 (4Q War Scroll$^g$)** consists of several fragments found in Cave 4. It is part of a document which has close affinities with 1QM and may even be part of the missing twentieth column of 1QM; it dates from the end of the first century BCE. Controversy arises over the reading of line 4 in Fragment 5 (on display in the exhibit). The first word of the line, *whmytw*, is vague and could be rendered either 'they kill the Prince of the Congregation' or 'the Prince of the Congregation kills him.' According to the first rendering, the Qumran sect expected the Messiah to be killed (by his enemies?); that would have significant implications for our understanding of the death of Jesus, the Messiah of early Jewish Christians. However, based on evidence from the immediate context and other Qumran documents (e.g. 4QpIs$^a$), most Scrolls scholars have opted for the second reading, which coincides with the sect's expectations of a triumphant Messiah Son of David, who is to judge and rule all nations in the endtime.

## 4QMMT$^{a-f}$ (4Q394-399)

4QMMT$^{a-f}$ signifies six highly fragmentary manuscripts which scholars think are copies of a single document. The title MMT represents an abbreviation of a Hebrew phrase, *Miqsat Ma'asey ha-Torah*, meaning 'some of the precepts of the law', which is found in one of these texts. They were copied at various points of time within the period 50 BCE - 20 CE.

Scholars have used these manuscripts to produce a composite text, about 130 lines long, which is believed largely to represent the original composition. The document contains three main types of material: calendrical material, halakhic rules (rules about practice) mainly about purity, and exhortations probably delivered by a leader of the movement to a certain leading figure in Israel, trying to persuade him of their teachings and urging him to part company with a third group here condemned as 'wicked'. This exhortative material leads many scholars to think that the document was originally in the form of a letter, although one of the two official editors responsible for editing and publishing these manuscripts claims it was a 'legal proclamation', not a letter.

The importance of this document 4QMMT is twofold. First, it sheds new light on the nature of the halakhic teaching of the sect. It has generally been considered that the Qumran sect was related to the Essenes, but some of the material in 4QMMT could be considered more closely related to what we know as Sadducean. On this basis, new theories have been advanced about the origins and history of the movement (see below, pp.39-42).

Secondly, 4QMMT is important to New Testament studies, especially the study of Paul. The document clearly spells out the conviction that one's righteousness before God is related to doing 'the works of the law', a phrase which seems equivalent to one used by Paul in his antithesis between 'works of the law' and 'faith in Christ'. Does this shed light on a common Jewish conviction, or only on a peculiarity of the Qumran community? Perhaps this document could reveal some important points of contrast between first century Judaism and the Pauline wing of the early Christian movement.

### The Thanksgiving Scroll (1QH)

This document, also called *Hodayot* from the Hebrew term for 'thanksgiving', is one of the seven scrolls found in cave 1 in 1947. It is a collection of psalms or hymns which express praise for God's mercy, protection, deliverance and revelation of truth. The hymns often begin with formulaic expressions such as 'I thank you, O Lord/my God' or 'Blessed are you, O Lord'. Most strike a strongly personal note, but it is difficult to ascertain whether they were originally composed for personal devotion or for corporate worship.

Due to the deterioration in the leather of the scroll, many of the hymns have become fragmentary and difficult to read. This makes it difficult to know when one hymn finishes and another begins, so the exact number collected in the scroll is a matter of guesswork. The script is early Herodian, so the scroll was copied at the end of the first century BCE; but some related fragments from Cave 4 suggest that the hymns were already composed by 100 BCE.

Who wrote these hymns? It has been suggested that some of the hymns, if not all, may be related to the mysterious leader of the Qumran community, the Teacher of Righteousness (e.g. the hymns in columns 2, 4 and 5). However, other scholars regard this suggestion with scepticism and consider the authorship indefinable and probably multiple.

The hymns collected in the scroll exhibit their writers' lavish use of Scripture, in form, imagery, vocabulary and concept. The psalmists' favourite scriptural sources were the Psalms and prophetic books, especially Isaiah. The hymns illustrate the beliefs of the movement very well, including their convictions about God's grace and election, predestination, and human sinfulness (see below, section 4).

### The Copper Scroll (3Q15)

This unique scroll was found in Cave 3 in 1952. As its name suggests, it is made of copper, not leather or papyrus, and it proved particularly difficult to read because of the severe oxidation of the material. Palaeographical analysis suggests a date after the mid first century CE: whether it was composed before or after the destruction of the Temple in 70 CE is a matter of debate. If the latter, it dates from after the destruction of the Qumran community, and may have been placed in the cave by someone else.

This scroll is one of the most fascinating and puzzling of the discoveries at the Dead Sea. It reads like a treasure-hunter's guide, describing treasures of an incredibly large quantity of gold and silver and their exact hiding-places. But this poses many difficult questions. Was this treasure anything to do with the Qumran sect? In view of the small size and isolation of the Qumran community, could they possibly have owned so much temple treasure? If so, how did they acquire it and how and when did they hide these treasures in more than sixty locations, both inside and outside Jerusalem? If the treasures were not the sect's property, how did this inventory get included among their relics? Does the Copper Scroll represent just one of the many treasure legends in antiquity? Such questions continue to trouble scholars and have led some to conclude that the document is merely a piece of 'fabulous folklore'.

However, the majority of scholars reject this conclusion, for two reasons. First, the writer's sober book-keeping style suggests that the treasure account was no mere fairy tale. Secondly, it is hard to explain why the writer chose such an expensive material, copper, to record the treasures if the account was just fanciful legend. The choice of this material demonstrates the writer's determination to keep the document from damage, which perhaps implies the genuineness of the account it contains. Despite our uncertainty here, many scholars now accept that the document really does derive from the Qumran community, and that the treasures it records were genuine - but probably already hunted by the Romans centuries ago!

### Calendars and Astrological Works

The distinctive calendar of the Qumran sect is well illustrated by **4Q Mishmarot B$^a$ (4Q321)**, copied in the second half of the first century BCE (on display). This delineates their calendar in terms of the weekly rotation of the twenty-four priestly divisions (Hebrew, *mishmarot*) described in 1 Chronicles 24, and was probably designed to guide their activities on the proper dates. The document shows an effort to synchronise their preferred 364-day solar calendar with the 354-day lunar calendar which was used by mainstream Judaism, although it is not altogether clear why such an effort should be made. Since calendrical computation may have been one of the factors which caused the Qumran community to break from Jewish society at large, this document is of some importance.

Another text with a special interest in the calendar is the badly preserved **Brontologion (4Q318)**, which seems to illustrate a method of predicting prodigies or bad omens by noting the occurrence of thunder on particular days of the month. There are also remarkable texts known as **Astrological Physiognomies (4Q186 and 534)** which claim a correspondence between people's physical features and destiny and the stellar configuration at the time of their birth. According to these intriguing texts, a tall, lean frame and long, thin toes denote a preponderance of aspects in 'the House of Light', whereas a fat build, hairiness and thick, short toes are among the characteristics of those who have the majority of their astrological 'houses' in the sphere of darkness. One of these horoscopes is of the birth of the Messiah, and predicts that he will have red hair and small birthmarks on his thigh! In the light of the fact that astrology is generally condemned in the Hebrew Bible, the presence of these manuscripts may seem surprising. But some Jews in antiquity (e.g. the writer Eupolemus) credited Abraham with its invention.

# 3    THE DEAD SEA SCROLLS AND QUMRAN

## Are the Dead Sea Scrolls related to the nearby buildings at Qumran?

Soon after the first scrolls were discovered in Cave 1 (see above, p.1), a nearby set of ruins (half a mile to the south) were briefly examined by archaeologists and some tombs opened, but no obvious connection was discovered with the material found in the caves. These ruins had long been known about, and it had been thought they were probably the remnants of a Roman fort. However, as the full significance of the scrolls material began to emerge, a full excavation of the site was undertaken by G L Harding and Roland de Vaux, from 1951 to 1956. Although the full final report of these excavations was never published, de Vaux produced a series of articles and a substantial book (*Archaeology and the Dead Sea Scrolls*, 1973) which set out his understanding of the site in full.

Roland de Vaux came to the conclusion, which has been shared by almost all scholars since, that the buildings at Qumran were indeed connected to the scrolls stored or hidden in the caves. Their sheer proximity is one factor in this conclusion, coupled with the fact that the date of the occupation of the site (see below) corresponds exactly with the date of the composition of the scrolls (see above pp.4-5). No scrolls were actually discovered in the Qumran ruins, but some writing was found there (e.g. a practice alphabet on a potsherd), together with inkwells in a room which de Vaux thought could be identified as a 'scriptorium' (writing room). Moreover, the pottery found on the site exactly corresponds in design and age to that found in the caves. Also, the site revealed a very great concern for purification (provision for sluicing out the dining room, and several immersion pools) which fits well the ideology of the scrolls, with their depiction of the Pure Meal and the Pure Community.

Thus most scholars consider it incontestable that the buildings at Qumran are connected to the scrolls and the people who put them in the caves. In recent years, however, a few dissident voices have been raised. Norman Golb has argued that the scrolls are the deposit of the Jerusalem temple, not of the people at Qumran, and that the buildings at Qumran were not settled by the authors or copiers of the scrolls but were a fortress. The first part of this thesis has a grain of plausibility: one might understand the authorities in Jerusalem hiding precious manuscripts in inaccessible places as the Romans advanced in 68 CE, and the Copper Scroll (see above, pp.27-28), which cryptically lists hiding places of treasures, has often been connected with Jerusalem. However, on Golb's hypothesis, it is hard to explain why such a large percentage of the manuscripts represent the distinctive views of only one of the many strands of first century Judaism: why are there no identifiably Pharisaic documents here, or ones we can link to the Sadducean authorities in the temple? The second part of the Golb-hypothesis, that the buildings were a fortress, is plainly wrong: although they include a small tower (for safe-keeping in times of crisis), they do not display the structure and defences one would expect in a fortress. Additional recent opinions that the buildings might be the ruins of a luxury villa, or a pottery workshop, or even a perfumery (!), are also unconvincing on archaeological grounds.

Thus the best hypothesis remains that of the consensus - that the Qumran buildings were used by those who put the scrolls in the adjacent caves. A recently published ostracon (potsherd), found in one of the walls of the buildings, may clinch this matter: it seems to have inscribed on it the word *yahad*, the distinctive for the community used in several scrolls.

## What buildings have been found at Qumran and when were they occupied?

R de Vaux's extended excavations at Qumran suggested two main phases of occupation, the first split into Ia and Ib. It remains hard to determine when Ia begins, but the evidence points to sometime in the second half of the second century BCE as the point of departure for this new settlement, which included kilns and cisterns to sustain the community. However, the community clearly expanded greatly around 130-100 BCE (the beginning of Phase Ib) and the buildings took on more or less the shape which we now see. These include:

⇒ elaborate water systems, such as an aqueduct, collecting water as it floods down the Wadi Qumran, several large cisterns, lined with plaster, and pools with steps, probably immersion pools for ritual cleansing;

⇒ a two-story tower (entered on the second story by a wooden bridge), clearly for emergency purposes only;

⇒ a large dining room, linked to the water system for ease of cleaning, and whose adjoining room contained over 1000 plates, bowls, jugs etc. Some bone deposits reveal what the occupants ate, including lamb, mutton, goat, veal and beef;

⇒ a large upper-story room, equipped with a table, a bench and at least two inkwells. As mentioned above, de Vaux identified this as a 'scriptorium', but some doubt this, not least because scribes usually wrote cross-legged, resting on their laps, not on tables;

⇒ a large room with benches around its walls, probably some kind of assembly room;

⇒ a kitchen and various kinds of workshops, though it is not . clear what they produced, apart from pottery.

At some stage this set of buildings was destroyed by an earthquake and a fire, and from the evidence of the coin deposits found in various parts of the building, de Vaux concluded that this took place in about 31 BCE (Josephus tells us there was an earthquake in that year; others think the destruction should be related to the invasion of Parthians in 40 BCE).

For some reason, the buildings were then unoccupied for a number of years, but were reactivated, in much the same form and usage, in about 4 CE (the start of Phase II). Coin evidence suggests that this stage lasted until 68 CE, when the buildings were destroyed, probably by Romans (did the community go out to battle thinking that God's final day of vengeance had begun?). Roman soldiers seem to have used parts of the building thereafter, and it may have been occupied again by Jews for a short while during the Second Revolt (132-135 CE), but basically 68 CE marks the end of the settlement founded in and around these buildings.

The excavated buildings do not include living quarters, which must have been in tents or caves in the vicinity. What we have at Qumran are the communal buildings of a desert community (perhaps numbering at most 250 at any one time) which eked out a very special form of existence by the Dead Sea.

## What cemeteries have been found at Qumran?

The main cemetery at Qumran is about 50m from the buildings (to the east) and contains about 1100 graves, neatly arranged on a north-south axis (head towards the south). R de Vaux excavated 26 of these and found the bodies all male, except in one case, an unusual grave physically set apart from the rest. However, in an extension of the cemetery, six graves were excavated, which included four female skeletons and one of a child. There were also what de Vaux called 'secondary cemeteries' to the north of the buildings and to the south of the Wadi, containing a few graves (about 15 and 30 respectively): only a few of these were opened, but they contained skeletons of both sexes, adult and child (though de Vaux reckoned very few of the people buried in these three cemeteries were over 40 years old).

These findings are important for their bearing on the make-up of the community at Qumran. Was it, as say some of our sources on the Essenes, an all-male celibate community, or did it include married members and their families? If the former, how did the children and female skeletons get there (visitors? from other branches of the same movement? local residents not part of the community?); if the latter, why is the most important and carefully arranged cemetery just about exclusively male (as far as we know)? It would be helpful if further excavations could be carried out to check the distribution of male and female skeletons. But the larger picture is confused further by the fact that some of the scrolls themselves presuppose married life (e.g. CD) or talk of the ideal priests as married (Temple Scroll, 4QMMT), and none explicitly requires celibacy. This then raises the question: should this community be identified with the Essenes?

## What is the relationship of the Qumran community to the Essenes?

Soon after the discovery of the Dead Sea Scrolls, most scholars concluded that we had at last discovered primary evidence for an otherwise obscure group which several ancient sources refer to as 'the Essenes'. In recent years, this hypothesis has come under sustained attack from a number of angles, to the extent that some scholars would deny any connection between Qumran and the Essenes and others would suggest only a distant relationship as a parallel phenomenon. Probably most Dead Sea Scrolls experts still hold to the identification of the Qumran community with (one branch of) the Essenes, but in order to understand this issue we need to break our question down into two parts: Who were the Essenes? and Were the people of Qumran Essenes?

1    Who were the Essenes?

The name 'Essenes' (which probably derives from one of two Aramaic words meaning 'healers' or 'pious ones') refers to a

Jewish religious community of the Second Temple period. We know about them from the writings of three first century CE authors: the Roman geographer Pliny the Elder, the Jewish philosopher Philo of Alexandria and the Jewish historian Flavius Josephus. All three characterise the Essenes as abstemious and devout.

Pliny locates the abode of the Essenes on the west side of the Dead Sea, above Engedi. He depicts them as living in self-imposed isolation, having renounced both women and money. Their numbers were maintained, he asserts, by a steady stream of men who, weary of life, yearned for a solitary existence with only palm trees for company.

Philo, estimating their number at about 4,000, describes the Essenes as living in villages, working at agriculture and dedicating much time to the communal study of moral and religious matters, including interpretation of their sacred books. He also refers to their scrupulous attention to ritual purity, common ownership of property, habitual celibacy and refusal to keep slaves, offer animal sacrifices, swear oaths, or take part in military or commercial activities.

Josephus lists the Essenes alongside the two other schools of Jewish philosophy (the Sadducees and Pharisees), and ascribes to them a formidable control of the passions and a rigorous eschewing of vice. He claims that they lived widely dispersed in every town and details their disdain for marriage (which is attributed to women's wantonness!). He indicates, however, that one order of Essenes did condone marriage for purposes of propagation, once prospective wives had gone through a three-year period of probation and purification. Further, the Essenes are described as despising opulence and sharing all possessions, as especially preoccupied with purity, and as believing in the immortality of the soul and in predestination.

It is clear that these three portraits have some things in common, though the discrepancy in location is striking: only Pliny locates them by the Dead Sea (Philo and Josephus in 'villages' or 'towns'). A degree of idealisation or exaggeration may affect the portrayal of these 'Essenes', and Josephus' knowledge of different kinds of Essene may indicate that the historical reality was multifarious or altered over time. Perhaps 'Essenism' was not a single or stable movement - a factor which has to be taken into account in the scholar's attempt to decide whether or not what we find at Qumran is related to the Essenes.

## 2    Were the people of Qumran Essenes?

From the evidence of the buildings and cemeteries alone, we would not have enough evidence to decide whose communal settlement this was. As noted above, Pliny refers to the presence of Essenes in this vicinity, but his geographical information is not exact; in any case, he was writing after the war of 66-73 CE, when the settlement was abandoned, while he describes the Essenes near Engedi in the present tense. Moreover, as noted above (pp.33-34), the presence of female and child skeletons in some outlying cemeteries could be taken to suggest that these are not his (or Philo's) male ascetics!

However, if the scrolls in the caves are linked to this settlement (see above, pp.30-32), we have a much richer, though rather varied, body of evidence to work with. It should be noted, first, that the name 'Essene' occurs nowhere in the scrolls, despite the very large number of documents now discovered. It is possible, of course, that the term was used by outsiders and not insiders. Such a discrepancy between insider and outsider terminology has often occurred in the history of religions, and it is common that those viewed by the mainstream as sectarians, and thus given a special label, view themselves as the mainstream, the true community, and thus decline to accept others' labels. The authors of those scrolls composed within the sect seem to have had a peculiar set of labels for themselves and for other Jews (and non-Jews), and might not have wished to use the term 'Essene'. Nonetheless, this discrepancy gives fuel to an increasing number of questions concerning the identification of this group.

Close scrutiny of the scrolls and of the classical sources on the Essenes reveals a number of points in which there appear to be discrepancies. For instance:

a) as we have seen, all three external sources stress the Essenes' celibacy. However, as well as the (marginal) presence of female and child skeletons in the cemeteries, some scrolls in the caves take a positive attitude to marriage. For instance, the Damascus Document mentions wives and children (e.g. it forbids a wet-nurse from lifting a baby to go out or come in on the Sabbath). The document known as 4QMMT (see above, pp.25-26) also presupposes that priests should marry. However, the Damascus Document might be related to that branch of the Essenes which Josephus mentions as sanctioning marriage, not necessarily that based at Qumran. This highlights the difficult question about the library in the caves: which of these works represent what actually was believed and practised at Qumran, and which were their 'reference works' representing a wider viewpoint? That is not an easy question to answer.

b) although both Josephus and the Community Rule mention a period of probation prior to admission, Josephus suggests this lasts three years, while the rule indicates two. However, the Community Rule can be interpreted in a way which tallies with Josephus' time-period - or Josephus might be mistaken, or the rule might have been modified over time. Again it is hard to tell which of these possibilities is more likely.

c) Josephus describes the unusual Essene practice of defecation, which involved (beside a ban on Sabbaths!) digging a small trench in a remote place with a special shovel. But in the Temple Scroll (11QTemple), no mention is made of this: defecation is secluded, but in walled and roofed facilities outside the settlement. Has Josephus exaggerated (or over-generalised from one special instance)? Or does the Temple Scroll describe an ideal for a city environment different from that practised at Qumran, and one where the holy city could hardly be defiled by carrying such shovels to and fro? Despite the differences in detail, the common anxiety about pollution from defecation is unparalleled in Judaism from this period.

These three examples, and the questions we have raised in relation to each, illustrate how difficult it is to know what we are comparing with what when we ask 'were the people at Qumran Essenes?' We do not know how accurate or representative are our outside sources on the Essenes, and we do not know what to make of the variety of material we find in the caves. Because of these uncertainties, it is possible for some scholars to hold to the consensus view that Qumran was a branch of the Essene movement, explaining differences as either inaccurate reporting in the outside sources, or signs of plurality or change in the Essene movement itself. But it is also possible for others to challenge the consensus, arguing that there are just too many inconsistencies between the scrolls and the evidence about the Essenes to make the identification reasonable. A large-scale scholarly battle is currently being waged on this point, whose outcome is by no means resolved.

Besides Pliny's geographical notice (locating Essenes on the west shore of the Dead Sea, above Engedi), there are at least three large issues which seem to place the people of Qumran in very close proximity to the Essene movement - either as a closely parallel phenomenon (unmentioned by any outside source) or, more likely, as a special phenomenon within a broader and variable Essenism. These three characteristics are:

a) regard for the sun: one of the distinctive features of many scrolls in the caves is their adoption of the solar calendar for calculating Jewish feasts and festivals. This must have set the movement at odds with most Jews, and especially with the Temple in Jerusalem, where a lunar calendar was followed, major festivals therefore occurring on different days in the year. Josephus suggests that the Essenes showed particular devotion to the sun (even praying at dawn, 'as though entreating him to rise') - which sounds like a garbled indication of the significance of the solar calendar within this movement.

b) communal life and common ownership of property: a rule-bound communal lifestyle and common ownership of property are regarded as typically Essene characteristics in the external sources, and are strikingly illustrated in the scrolls. The careful regulation of community life is well evidenced, for instance, in the Community Rule and the Damascus Document, while the pooling of resources is specifically detailed in the Community Rule. In describing the Essenes Josephus depicts the pure meal of the community, preceded by bathing, in terms quite similar to the meal regulations in the Community Rule. These are striking enough phenomena to suggest that the Qumran community is uncannily like what others describe as Essene.

c) Josephus describes Essene theology as influenced by predeterminism. Although his category is inexact and rhetorically shaped, this does accord extremely well with the strong sense of fate, lot and divine election which is such a striking feature of many of the scrolls (see below, pp.63-64).

There is no doubt that the early scholarly consensus that the Qumran people were Essenes needs to be re-examined, and at the very least qualified in certain respects, in the light of the material which has only recently been made public. The sheer variety of this material raises all sorts of questions concerning the status of the texts in the caves, since no-one could believe and practise all the things in those texts at the same time! Perhaps the consensus will change, or perhaps there will never be a consensus again, but for the moment it still looks most likely that the Qumran community was a special manifestation of a larger (somewhat variable) Essene movement, or at least a special settlement with close affinities to those our external sources describe, with varying degrees of accuracy, as Essenes.

## What was the history of this community?

This is an extremely difficult question to answer, in fact, one becoming harder and harder the more material from the caves is published! Even a confident identification of the Qumran community with the Essenes would not help us, since our sources say nothing of their origins or history, and they do not appear in our other, somewhat scanty, sources on the history of Judaism in this period. Thus we are driven to the internal evidence of the scrolls themselves which are:

a) often cryptic in their references to places (e.g. is 'Damascus' a real or a symbolic location?), times (are their chronologies numbered realistically or only symbolically?) and people (e.g. references to 'the Wicked Priest' and 'the Man of the Lie');

b) not obviously consistent in the narrative they tell. In particular, it is hard to place newly published works, like 4QMMT, within the saga implied by other sources: does this come from an earlier stage, or from a different, but related, group?

Most scholars are learning to be less confident than they once were in reconstructing the history of the Qumran group and explaining how it came to be where it is. Its origins probably lie in the turbulent years of the second century BCE when the attempt of some priests to 'Hellenise' Jerusalem and the Temple cult resulted in the backlash of the Maccabean revolt (175-167 BCE). As a result, a number of shifting internal factions grew up within Judaism, centred on the priesthood, the conduct of the Temple cult and the proper interpretation of the law of Moses. Religion and politics were here closely intertwined, and when the Hasmoneans (the descendants of the Maccabean victors) were appointed high-priests, they easily fell foul of the competing factions within the Jewish nation.

The recently published 4QMMT is a curious document which urges a leader in Israel to take note of one group's interpretation of the law (especially regarding Jerusalem) and to follow it, rather than any rival views. This document may belong to an early stage in the history of the movement, when they have begun to break away from the mainstream ('we have separated ourselves from the multitude of the people'), but still hope to persuade others, whom they refer to without vituperation. The editors tentatively date this document to 159-152 BCE and consider that it may have been addressed to Jonathan Maccabaeus, who ruled at that time and was appointed high-priest in 152.

However, other texts at Qumran talk of a huge rift between the community, led by 'the Teacher of Righteousness', and a priestly figure dubbed 'the Wicked Priest' (some think this is a composite symbol, referring to many different priests). The pesher to Habakkuk suggests an early appreciation for this person which turned sour: 'he was called by the true name at the beginning of his course, but when he ruled in Israel he became arrogant, abandoned God and betrayed the statutes for the sake of wealth' (1QpHab8:9-13). It is also reported that the Wicked Priest

> pursued the Teacher of Righteousness to the house of his exile that he might confuse him with his venomous fury. And at the time appointed for rest, for the Day of Atonement, he appeared before them to confuse them, and to cause them to stumble on the Day of Fasting, their Sabbath of repose.' (1QpHab11:4-9)

It is not clear what this represents, but it is possible that a difference in calendar is one factor in this breach, the Teacher's Day of Atonement falling on a different day than the Priest's (the Teacher probably followed a solar rather than a lunar calendar). The reference to 'exile' suggests a decisive split taking shape at this point, and this may have been a precipitating moment in the self-definition of the Teacher's community as a 'new covenant', the true Israel.

Here and elsewhere it is implied that the Teacher was himself a priest and many think he was the loser in a power-struggle within the priestly hierarchy. Certainly, the ideology of the subsequent texts which look back to him is heavily priestly, and the community is often described as led by 'sons of Zadok' (the priestly dynasty). In some of its interpretations of the law, 4QMMT lies very close to what much later rabbinic texts describe as 'Sadducean' viewpoints, leading some scholars to describe the whole movement as a Sadducean phenomenon (the term

Sadducee derives from the name Zadok). However, the label 'Sadducean' can have both broad and narrow meanings: in the broad sense the roots of Qumran may lie in priestly (Zadokite) opinions on the purity of the Temple and the priesthood, but in the narrow sense of the aristocratic Hellenizing party which compromised with Rome (the sense used by Josephus and the New Testament) there is clearly a large gulf between Qumran and such 'Sadducees'.

Just as labels can be differentially applied, or can shift in meaning over time, so it may be that the movement we find represented at Qumran had its roots in Jerusalem controversies and links to various analogous or related movements but no single or simple line of development. The truth is that we do not know why the settlement at Qumran went through periods of expansion and a period of abandonment (see above, pp.32-33). Nor can we yet make sense of the variety of documents preserved, copied and hidden in the various caves, which not only seem to describe different kinds of community (e.g. the differences between the Community Rule and the Damascus Document) but also display a variety of perspectives, some narrowly sectarian in character, others with little obvious relation to a self-conscious sect. Whether these reflect different stages in the history of one and the same movement, different branches of a broadly-defined movement, or the breadth of resources used by a narrowly-based group is a matter which scholars will continue to debate for a long time to come.

## What was it like to live in the Qumran community?

### Imagining the experience

In order to gain an idea of what it was like to be a member of the Qumran community, it may be helpful to imagine the experience of a first-century Jew who joined the sect. Let's call him Mordechai ben Joshua, and let's listen to his account of his experiences from the time that he first heard about the community, through his period of initiation, probation, and acceptance as a fully-fledged member, and on into his subsequent life in the sect. (For the benefit of the modern reader, the 'editor' of Mordechai's account has inserted references to scroll columns and line numbers in parentheses. The 'editor' also suggests that Mordechai's writing should be dated to around 80 CE.)

### First contact

As a young man, I shopped around spiritually; like the great historian Josephus (*Life* 7-12) and other Jews, I investigated and even temporarily joined several of the sects that existed in such profusion before our war with Rome destroyed all but one of them, the Pharisees. For a few years I myself was a Pharisee, attracted to that sect by its stress on ritual purity and the concern its members displayed for one another (cf. Josephus, *Jewish War* 2.166). But eventually I became dissatisfied with the Pharisees. Their purity regulations and other traditions, while stricter than those of the common run of Jews, seemed to me to make too many compromises with human frailty. They were 'seekers after smooth things', to adopt the terminology that I later learned to use when I became a member of the Qumran community (e.g. CD 1:18). I craved something more than the Pharisees had to offer: a more intense communal life, a greater purity, a higher righteousness.

Then, one day, while walking through the section of Jerusalem known as the Essene Quarter, I fell into conversation with a serious-looking stranger who told me his name was Eliezer. When our discussion turned to the Law of Moses and its proper interpretation, which was a matter of great controversy amongst us Jews at that time, he spoke with a wisdom and authority that amazed me. Somehow, this sense of authority induced me to confide in him, and to my own amazement I found myself revealing my most closely-guarded secret: the sense of spiritual emptiness that haunted my life.

'Then have you not found the Way yet, brother?' Eliezer asked.

'The Way?  Which way are you talking about?'

'The Way of the Lord, of which the prophet Isaiah spoke when he said, "In the wilderness prepare the Way of the Lord" (Isa 40:3; cf. 1QS 8:13-16).  I am a member of a holy fellowship that seeks to follow in that Way.'

'What fellowship is that?'

'I care not what foolish outsiders may call us.  We call ourselves "The One" or "The Unity", because we live at one with each other and with the Lord, and "the Children of Light", because God has shined the light of His holy law into our hearts. We pursue a life of sanctity, love, and righteousness, following the interpretation of the Law of Moses that was bequeathed to us by our founder, the great Teacher of Righteousness, may his name be blessed.'

'But where do you live this holy life?  And might a stranger be granted the chance to experience it?'

'We are scattered all over the land of Israel.  Some of us live in Jerusalem, the holy city - but a city, alas, that now wallows in impurity as a result of the usurpation of the Temple by a corrupt priesthood.  Others dwell in towns and villages throughout Israel, following the interpretation of the Law of Moses laid down in one of the sacred rulebooks of our Way, the Damascus Document (see CD 12:19 and cf. Josephus, *Jewish War*, 2.160 on two orders of Essenes).  But the stricter portion of our holy brotherhood, the portion that aspires to greater holiness, follows the instruction of Isaiah and our great Teacher's example by preparing the Way of the Lord in the wilderness.  There we devote our lives to Torah study, purity, and communal fellowship in a settlement by the Dead Sea.  This group of pious ones walks according to the interpretation of the Law set out in another of our holy books, the Community Rule.'

My heart burned within me as I listened to Eliezer, and I begged him to show me this holy settlement in the wilderness. 'God's mysteries are only for His elect,' he replied, 'and may not be revealed to strangers. But perhaps, on second thoughts, you *are* one of the elect, Mordechai. Perhaps you are not really a stranger but a child of Light. Somehow I feel that you may be. If you wish it, then, I will bring you to the one whom we call the Examiner, the leader of our community.'

'I wish it with all my heart.'

'But first let me warn you: as his title implies, the Examiner has the power to see into men's souls. If you are coming to spy on our holy mysteries for some unworthy purpose, he will detect it, and then the judgement on you will be fearful.'

'I do not come for any such purpose, but out of a great thirst to be instructed in the mysteries of the Law.'

## Initiation

A few days later, I stood in fear and trembling before the Examiner. He inquired about my past life; he tested my understanding of the Law. But more searching than this verbal examination was another, silent interrogation that was occurring simultaneously. I felt his eyes boring into my soul, and my every secret sin, in all its grotesque ugliness, being revealed to his gaze. And then, just when I was sure that I would be rejected, forever shut out from the regions of day, I heard him say, 'You are a child of the Light!' And there and then he began to instruct me in the ordinances of the Community, indicating that I had been granted the grace to enter the holy covenant (1QS 6:13-15).

He then took me by the hand and led me to the Council of the Congregation, where I was received as a brother. In this Council the Examiner was assisted by a 'cabinet' of three priests and twelve laymen (1QS 8:1-4). There were also, I found out, other functionaries in the community, for example a Bursar who was in charge of material needs. Indeed, the community as a whole seemed extremely well-ordered; the congregation sat arranged in groups, 'by thousands and hundreds and tens' (1QS 2:21; CD 13:1; 1QSa 1:14-15) - though 'thousands' is a bit of an exaggeration; as far as I saw, there were never more than 250 or so people living at Qumran at any one time. But this language recalls the organisation of the children of Israel in their wilderness wanderings under Moses, the golden era of our Jewish history, and the pattern for our coming redemption (Exodus 18:21, 25; Deuteronomy 1:15).

Within these 'thousands, hundreds, and tens' the holy congregation was further subdivided in accordance with God's purpose. First in order of precedence were the priests, including the Examiner himself. Even amongst them there was a division, for precedence was given to those priests who were 'sons of Zadok', i.e. from the legitimate high-priestly line, as the Examiner was, as all the Examiners before him had been, and as our founder, the Teacher of Righteousness, had been before them. After the priests came the Levites (a group of families that traditionally served as attendants in the Temple), then ordinary Israelites, and finally proselytes to Judaism. Yes, we even had some people in our holy fellowship who had been born as godless Gentiles (CD 14:3-4; 11QTemple 39:5-7).

And so I entered the covenant community, the One; I embarked upon the Way, vowing 'by a binding oath to return with all [my] heart and soul to every commandment of the Law of Moses in accordance with all that has been revealed of it to the sons of Zadok, the Priests, the Keepers of the Covenant' (1QS 5:7-11).

### Probation

But I did not immediately become a fully-fledged member; I could not yet join in the pure Meal of the Unity, but had to eat separately so as not to defile the other brothers. That was a trial to me - so close, and yet so far away! But I gradually realised the wisdom of this regulation. One cannot so easily cast off the works of darkness, and many who began the course did not persevere to the end but were waylaid by the devil, whom we call Belial - thus revealing that they had never really been children of Light in the first place. And so our founder, the Teacher of

Righteousness, wisely decreed that there should be a period of probation for new members of the community.

This probation proceeded in stages. After the first year, I 'mingled my property with the Many' in a preliminary way, turning over to the Bursar all my worldly possessions (1QS 3:17). At Qumran all things were held in common and no one owned personal property, and the donations of members' possessions, along with communal agriculture, were our chief means of supporting ourselves. (We supported ourselves rather well, too, I may say; as a matter of fact, I suspect that some 'inquirers' were attracted to Qumran as much by the promise of obtaining plentiful food as they were by the hope of receiving spiritual nourishment. I'm sure that the Examiner saw through these frauds, and only let them remain so that their subsequent apostasy should become an object-lesson to those of us who were truly chosen.)

But my donation of my goods at the end of a year did not mean that I was irrevocably joined to the Community yet. The Bursar gave me a receipt for my property, and told me that at any time before the end of the second year I could claim a full refund and depart with no questions asked. I didn't, of course. To exchange the realm of God's light and love for filthy lucre? What sort of madman would do that? I persevered, and after two years I finally became a full member of the Covenant community.

### Purity, Bathing, and Common Meal

I shall never forget that day, a day that I had been anticipating for two long years; in a deeper sense, indeed, it seemed that I had been looking forward to it all my life. At a meeting of the full congregation in the great assembly hall, my property was irrevocably mingled with that of the Community; I ceremonially burnt the Bursar's receipt, and with it my bridges back to the world of darkness and sin. Then I stood once again under the piercing gaze of the Examiner; he looked into my soul, weighing its proportion of light and of darkness, and assigning me a rank in accordance with that proportion. Everyone in the Community was weighed yearly in this manner, and the Examiner's ranking established an absolute order of precedence: a man had always to obey those above him in rank, to wait for them to speak first, and so on (1QS 5:23; 6:10-13, 26). I was, I have to admit, a bit let down to be assigned the ninety-sixth ranking in the pecking order, especially since the community consisted of only ninety-eight members at the time; but this momentary disappointment was quickly vanquished by the reflection that the Examiner undoubtedly knew best. Besides, I was soon swept up in the joy of my first experience of the pure food of the community.

As I have already indicated, a desire to attain a higher level of purity was one of the things that had attracted me to the Qumran community in the first place. This concern for ritual purity at Qumran was expressed in a thousand different ways. At Qumran, for example, defecation was treated as a defiling activity, whereas other Jews did not do so (see above, p.37). Oil was banned, since it was considered to be a good "conductor" of impurity (CD 12:15-17; cf. Josephus, *Jewish War* 2.123); similarly, it was believed that a stream of liquid transmitted the impurity from an unclean container back to a clean one (4QMMT 55-58). Although no one ever explained it to me, I assume that the stringent prohibition on spitting reflected a similar anxiety (1QS 7:13). This concern with ritual purity is part of the explanation for the fact that dealings with women were minimised, since unfortunately women are a natural source of ritual contagion.

The Qumran concern with purity, however, was most clearly expressed in the rules for eating. This is logical, since in eating a person takes a foreign substance into his body; if that substance is unclean, he himself becomes defiled. Therefore, to protect the Community from defilement, our Lawgiver, the Teacher of Righteousness, did not allow those on probation, who were still ritually unclean, to touch the plates, pots, or bowls that the full members used, nor to eat in company with the rest of the Community. This concern for ritual purity in eating also explains the fact that fully-fledged Community members, before they ate, had to bathe their bodies with water - which is why there was a

**PLATE 1** View of Wadi Qumran and Cave 4
Though the terrain appears arid, in the wet season water rushing down the wadi would have been trapped in cisterns to supply the community.

**PLATE 2** The complex of buildings at Qumran, looking west towards the Wadi.

**PLATE 3**  Steps leading down to a cistern which may have served as a ritual bath for members of the community.

**PLATE 4**  Site of the probable *Scriptorium*, where evidence has been found of writing materials and arrangements for scribes to carry on their work.

**PLATE 5**  The Dead Sea viewed from Masada.
The capture of the stronghold of Masada by the Romans in 73 CE marked the final end of the revolt of 66. Qumran, about 60 kilometres to the north, was probably destroyed about 68 CE.

**PLATE 6**  The Roman camp at the foot of Masada, from which the siege was mounted.

**PLATE 7** The Western ('Wailing') Wall in Jerusalem, with the Dome of the Rock above.

Two aspects of the religious plurality of modern Jerusalem (Judaism, Christianity and Islam in their many forms): a reminder that the diversity of belief indicated by the Dead Sea Scrolls is a constant theme in this land.

**PLATE 8** The Old City viewed through the window of the Church of Dominus Flevit ('Jesus wept') on the Mount of Olives.

**ACKNOWLEDGMENTS**
1 & 3: Joel Marcus;  2 & 4: Diana Barclay;  5 & 6: Maggie Hunter;  7 & 8: Alastair Hunter

ritual bathing pool situated right at the entrance of the assembly hall where meals were taken.

How well I remember my first ritual bath at Qumran, and the common meal that followed. I went down the steep steps into the cistern, and as I entered for the first time into the pure rainwater collected in that sacred pool, I felt a wave of holy power pass through my body, in fulfilment of the wonderful promise of spiritual cleansing contained in our Community Rule (see the quotation from 1QS 3:7-9 on p.70 below). For the first time in my life, I felt truly *clean* - cleansed of my sins, freed of every trace of ritual impurity, innocent as a new Adam suddenly set down on a freshly-created earth by a loving God.

I fairly flew out of the bath and into the assembly hall, where an impressive silence reigned, though the hall was almost full - remember, I was the low man in the pecking order, so nearly everyone had bathed and grouped themselves around tables before I entered. All of our meals, of course, were taken communally; there was no such thing at Qumran as raiding the pantry late at night. As the Community Rule specifies, 'They shall eat in common and bless in common and deliberate in common' (1QS 6:2-3). And even though I was suddenly faint with hunger and with the excitement of the day's momentous events (I had fasted for three days to sharpen my spiritual wits for the occasion), I dared not reach out my hand to eat anything. For as our sacred Community Rule again declares:

When the table has been prepared for eating, and the new wine for drinking, the Priest shall be the first to stretch out his hand to bless the first-fruits of the bread and new wine     1QS 6:4-5

I waited, then, until the Priest - that is, the Examiner - had blessed the bread and wine and partaken of a small amount of each, before I reached out my own hand to bless and eat. And I reflected, as I did so, that just as I had tarried for the Examiner, so in the swiftly-approaching Age to Come I would wait for the great Messiah, the son of Aaron, to stretch out his hand, bless the bread and wine, and eat (see 1QSa 2:17-21). What a great privilege - to eat in the presence of the Messiah of Aaron, and even now to have, in the pure Meal of the Community, a foretaste of that coming feast in the kingdom of God!

I had been through two long, hard years of probation. I had sacrificed all my worldly goods to the community treasury and had cut off all contact with my physical family, who had tried by persuasion and threats to get me to return to Jerusalem. Yet my new, spiritual family had not up to this point been willing to accept me completely either; I had endured the solitude of having to eat my meals alone, and had experienced deep shame at my ritual uncleanness when prohibited from touching the dishes that the others used. I had not had an easy time. But that evening, as I tasted the pure bread of Unity and drank the new wine of the coming age, as I felt myself taken into joyful communion with the other brothers and with the God whose grace seemed to pulse through that blessed hall in waves of radiant holiness - I realised that it had all been worth it.

### Discipline

I must admit, however, that I had some second thoughts in the next few weeks. The man immediately ahead of me in the pecking order, Shlomo ben Gedaliah, was making my life miserable by ordering me about like a slave, taking advantage of provisions in our holy rule that require that a community member obey every order that comes from a higher-ranking brother (1QS 5:23; 6:25-27). Other rules, to be sure, say that a man should love his brother as himself, seek his brother's good, and bear no rancour against him (CD 6:20-7:3), all of which Shlomo was constantly flaunting by his malicious harassment.

One day, however, he overstepped himself. We were filing into the holy assembly hall in rank order for the evening meal, when I tripped and inadvertently bumped into him.

'Watch out, you stupid son of Belial!' he snapped, loud enough for everyone in the assembly hall to hear.

'Who spoke?' rang out the voice of our Examiner.

Shlomo ben Gedaliah cleared his throat. Well, I thought, perhaps I have misjudged him. At least he is going to admit what he has done.

'Master, I must be candid - it was the new brother, Mordechai ben Joshua!'

What! Not only to insult me publicly, but also to shift the blame onto me! I couldn't believe it.

But Shlomo had not reckoned with the divine wisdom of the Examiner, who knows all that goes on and sees into the souls of men.

'Shlomo ben Gedaliah, stand forth!' he cried.

Shlomo took a step forward.

'Our holy rule says that the man who deliberately insults his companion shall do penance for one year and be excluded from the pure Meal of the Congregation for that time. And it says that the man who deliberately lies shall do penance for sixth months (1QS 7:3-5). You have insulted your brother, and you have lied. The eye of God sees all; the hand of God is swift to punish. You shall do penance for one-and-a-half years, and you shall be excluded from our pure Meal for one year. Reflect on the power of God!'

I was so relieved and happy that I couldn't help laughing out loud.

'And you, Mordechai ben Joshua,' the Examiner added, 'shall do penance for thirty days for that foolish guffaw' (1QS 7:16).

That didn't sound so bad at first - I thought that 'penance' just meant saying you were sorry, or reciting some penitential prayers. I soon found out that it was a bit more serious than that: it meant having your food rations cut by twenty-five per cent.

Many other transgressions and their punishments were detailed in our Community Rule. My sentence of a month's 'penance' was relatively light, the same punishment that was dealt out for falling asleep or spitting in the Assembly, or for letting one's nakedness appear 'when drawing his hand from beneath his garment' (1QS 7:10, 13-14; I was never sure exactly what that last provision meant, and I didn't like to ask). More serious was the punishment that Shlomo received, exclusion from the pure Meal of the community, which effectively demoted him to the level of one on probation; this penalty was also used for transgressions such as refusing to obey a higher-ranking brother's order, speaking in anger against one of the priests, or slandering a brother (1QS 7:3-4, 15-16).

Most serious of all were the heinous offences that resulted in permanent excommunication from the Community: blasphemy, murmuring against the Community's authority, or betraying its secrets (1QS 7:1-2, 17, 23). The person who had committed such offences was drummed out with terrible curses, which were intoned by the priests and Levites:

Cursed be the man ... who sets up before himself his stumbling-block of sin so that he may backslide ... God's wrath and His zeal for His precepts shall consume him in everlasting destruction. All the curses of the Covenant shall cling to him and God will set him apart for evil. He shall be cut off from the midst of all the sons of light, and...his lot shall be among those who are cursed for ever.                                    1QS 2:11-18

### Worship and Calendar

Although my punishment fell far short of excommunication, I found it difficult enough, and to my shame I must confess that I even briefly considered leaving the holy Way. I was sustained through this difficult period, however, by the wonderful worship of our Community. Each day, at morning and evening - the times devoted to sacrifice in the Temple in Jerusalem - we filed into the assembly hall for our prayers. The Temple itself might be defiled, but within our Community pure worship of God was still taking place, and so lofty was that worship that it seemed that God's holy angels were joining in our worship, and we in theirs (cf. the Songs for the Holocaust of the Sabbath).

The service began with a beautiful hymn to the power of God displayed in creation:

[I will praise God] at the times ordained by Him:
At the beginning of the dominion of light,
and at its end when it returns to its appointed place;
at the beginning of the watches of darkness when He unlocks
      their storehouse and spreads them out,
and also at their end when they retire before the light.

1QS 10:1-3

This hymn describes the regular progression of the heavenly bodies, the daily appearance, disappearance, and reappearance of the sun, moon, and stars, as testimony to God's purposeful guidance of the universe. And the constant renewal of these heavenly luminaries hints that the era of Satanic darkness, evil, and death is about to give way to the dominion of light.

This sort of cosmic mysticism helps to explain why the calendar was so important to us at Qumran. By observing the festivals at their proper times according to the movements of the heavenly bodies, we were ordering our lives in harmony with the God who guides those bodies safely in their courses through the vastness of space. Unlike 'the transgressors of the covenant', i.e. other Jews, who observed a lunar calendar, we followed one based on the solar year. The superiority of this solar calendar and its harmony with the God of the universe are easily discernible in the fact that all of the festivals fall out on the same day of the week each year, whereas according to the lunar calendar they fall on different days. Our use of a different calendar also explains how, near the beginning of our history, the Wicked Priest from Jerusalem managed to attack our Teacher of Righteousness on the Day of Atonement, when all Jews are supposed to fast and pray, and none is supposed to work, much less launch a military assault (1QpHab 11:2-8): it was the Day of Atonement for the Teacher of Righteousness, who was following the correct solar calendar, but not for the Wicked Priest, who was following the sinful lunar calendar.

Besides showing us the true calendar, God also revealed to us that, in these last days before the end, we were to add two new pilgrimage festivals to those prescribed in the Bible: a festival of new wine and a festival of new oil (11QTemple 19 and 22). Although none of our sacred writings said so explicitly, I was given to understand that these additional festivals pointed forward to the swiftly-approaching redemption, when we would drink new wine and be anointed with the oil of gladness in the kingdom of God.

### Epilogue

But what has happened now to all these fond hopes of redemption? As I write, Jerusalem lies in ruins, devastated in the Jewish revolt against the Romans (66-73 CE), a conflict that we thought was the beginning of the final War of the Children of Light against the Children of Darkness. Instead it turned out to be the end of our Community of the Children of Light; in the midst of the conflict, the Qumran settlement was destroyed and the site was turned into a Roman fort. Most of our holy brotherhood was either killed or scattered to the four winds. Some of those who were spared completely lost their faith in the coming redemption, while others kept it but wandered into ways of apostasy, such as the strange and offensive new doctrine that proclaims a crucified man, a transgressor of the Law, to be God's Messiah.

At least I managed, with the help of a few of the brothers, to hide our entire library of sacred scrolls in the caves that dot the hillsides near Qumran before the Romans came. But now, ten years later, I lie on my deathbed as I pen these words, and there are no successors to carry on my work. But perhaps someday someone will find our holy scrolls again, and the prophecy contained in our glorious Community Rule will be fulfilled: 'Then truth, which had wallowed in the ways of wickedness during the dominion of falsehood until the appointed time of judgment, shall arise in the world for ever' (1QS 4:19-20).

Amen, let it be so; fulfil your holy prophecy, O Lord, at the time that seems best to you, in the inscrutable depths of your marvellous wisdom.

*The words of Mordechai the son of Joshua are ended.*

## What are the most important aspects of the discovery of the Dead Sea Scrolls?

From antiquarian, historical and ideological points of view the importance of the scrolls would seem to be a multitude of things. From the point of view of biblical and Jewish studies the scrolls are fundamentally important for the study of ancient texts. They are the oldest set of biblical texts yet discovered (previously 850 CE) and they fill a gap between the production of the Hebrew Bible and the writing of the Mishnah (the earliest codification of rabbinic halakhah). Textual criticism and linguistic studies have benefited greatly from the discovery of the scrolls. From a Christian origins point of view they appear to provide some necessary background information towards understanding the social and religious character of the Jewish background out of which the Christian communities emerged. The scrolls also illustrate some of the kinds of scriptural interpretation techniques which can be found in the New Testament. Thus, for example, John's Gospel now looks so much more like having a Jewish background than once was thought to be the case before the discovery of the scrolls.

From the point of view of how texts are received, read and interpreted, the discovery of the Dead Sea Scrolls has been of enormous importance because it has demonstrated yet again the extent to which, both now and in ancient times, interpretation is a shared function of communities. The Qumran community read their scriptures in accordance with their views of the Jerusalem regime and their messianic hopes. Similarly, modern people have found in the scrolls what they wished to find there and have interpreted them in their own image. At the same time the scrolls have provided scholars with invaluable palaeographic information about the prehistory of much of the literature which subsequently became incorporated into the Hebrew Scriptures (and to some extent into the Christian Bible).

### Are there esoteric mysteries hidden in the scrolls?

Yes, if readers believe in that sort of thing. No, if readers do not think that way. The answers to all such questions about 'the meaning of life and its secret codes' are invariably provided in agreement with prior beliefs rather than in dependence on such happenstance occurrences as the discovery of the scrolls.

If readers believe, think or are convinced that somewhere there is a secret, a code, a book, a diet, a habit, a way of life, a discovery waiting to be made, a religion to be joined or followed or a formula waiting to be discovered, and that once it has been obtained, discovered, revealed or encountered everything will slip into place and the secrets of the universe and a successful life(style) will become available to the believers, then Yes the scrolls may well provide such an elixir of life, the holy Grail, for which all believers earnestly search throughout their lives.

On the other hand, if no such beliefs are entertained about the scrolls or about the Essenes (and if their connection with the Dead Sea Scrolls is disputed or denied), then the Scrolls will not be perceived to contain arcane matters bearing on the interpretation and revelation of the secrets of the universe. We may then be soberly content to appreciate the more down-to-earth, but no less exciting ways in which the Dead Sea Scrolls have helped to shed light on one corner of a past which is of interest to so many people.

# 4 THE SIGNIFICANCE OF THE DEAD SEA SCROLLS FOR UNDERSTANDING ANCIENT JUDAISM

## What do the scrolls reveal about the text of the Hebrew Bible (Old Testament)?

The variety of textual traditions evident amongst the Dead Sea Scrolls indicates that at the time when they were being produced there was no single, fixed and authoritative text. When we remember that the Old Testament tells of events and people stretching back (in some instances) 1200 years or so prior to its writing, this presents some problems. If the Book of Samuel, which deals with the period prior to 1000 BCE, is uncertain in form, as the scrolls seem to suggest (4QSam[a] contains a passage not preserved in the Masoretic Text), how far can we rely on other biblical texts for factual accuracy? (See also the Jeremiah scroll discussed above, pp.14-15). We may in fact be seeing evidence of traditions which were still developing as late as the time of Jesus.

This possibility is particularly striking in the case of Psalms. The scroll 11QPs[a] contains both psalms material not found in the Bible, and a quite different ordering of biblical psalms - suggesting that at the time of its composition the collection was still open to amendment and addition. In short, we might be justified in concluding that as late as the first century BCE this was a living, vital tradition. Of course, if the community associated with Qumran was separated from mainstream Temple worship, what we see in this scroll may be a sectarian alternative to the 'authorised' hymn book of the Temple.

At the level of detailed study of the text, several interesting observations result from studying the scrolls. First, the character of the divine name in Biblical Hebrew has long been known to be special. The four letters (the *Tetragrammaton*) YHWH which occur frequently in the Hebrew text are never vocalised. Instead the reader is directed to enunciate the word *adonai* which means 'Lord'. Examination of the scrolls reveals that these letters are often written in a deliberately old-fashioned script, or in some cases not written at all - merely indicated by means of four non-alphabetic marks on the page: interesting confirmation of the antiquity of this tradition of intense respect for the divine name.

Secondly, the scrolls provide evidence for various scholarly techniques for analysing (and proposing amendments to) the Hebrew text. Chapter 40 of the Isaiah Scroll 1QIsa$^a$ displays (a) a passage seemingly omitted by accident and written in along the margin; (b) corrected words above the line; and (c) words in the body of the text which are different from those in the Masoretic Text, but which had been previously proposed by scholars as suitable emendations for problematic terms in the traditional text.

It is clear that both as regards larger issues, and as regards the minutiae of the biblical texts, the Dead Sea Scrolls provide an invaluable window into the history and accuracy of what we know as the Old Testament.

## What do the scrolls reveal about the canon of the Hebrew Bible?

It is doubtful if it is appropriate to speak of a *canon* of scripture before the Christian period. Early controversies in Christianity led ultimately to the definition of an authorised collection of books (the New Testament) which formed part of the biblical canon for the Church. The Hebrew Bible is equally problematic, since there is evidence that debates about which books should be included continued in Jewish circles well into the second century CE.

As a rule of thumb, scholars have proposed that 'scriptures' which are quoted as authorities in non-scriptural scrolls might be considered 'canonical', with the proviso that this is a technical term which may not be strictly appropriate. Five secondary Qumran texts have been analysed for their use of scriptural texts, and the results are given in the table below:

| Genesis | CD | Exodus | 1QS, CD (2) 4QFlor | Leviticus | CD (4) 11QMelch (2) |
|---|---|---|---|---|---|
| Numbers | CD (4) 1QM 4QTestim | Deuteronomy | CD (8) 4QTestim (2) 11QMelch | | |
| Joshua | 4QTestim | Judges | | 1-2 Samuel | CD (?) 4QFlor (2) |
| 1-2 Kings | | Isaiah | 1QS (2) CD (6) 1QM, 4QFlor 11QMelch (3) | Jeremiah | |
| Ezekiel | CD (3) 4QFlor | Hosea | CD (3) | Joel | |
| Amos | CD (2) 4QFlor | Obadiah | | Jonah | |
| Micah | CD (4) | Nahum | | Habakkuk | |
| Zephaniah | | Haggai | | Zechariah | CD |
| Malachi | 4QFlor, 11QMelch (3) | | | | |
| Psalms | 4QFlor (2) 11QMelch (3) | Proverbs | CD | Job | |
| Song of Solomon | | Ruth | | Lamentations | |
| Ecclesiastes | | Esther | | Daniel | 4QFlor, 11QMelch |
| Ezra | | Nehemiah | | 1-2 Chronicles | |

If Qumran commentaries on scripture are also included, we could add Zephaniah and Habakkuk to the collection. Unfortunately, this is merely negative evidence, and does not really take us to a robust conclusion. Further, on the same principle, certain non-biblical texts - Jubilees (of which 15 or 16 copies have been found amongst the scrolls), 1 Enoch and the Temple Scroll - would merit the status of canonical texts at Qumran.

In short, while we can confirm the *existence* of most of the Hebrew Bible amongst the scrolls, we must conclude that the question of canon remains open. Indeed, we might be wiser to interpret the evidence as pointing to the likelihood that 'canon' is not really an issue or a coherent concept before the Christian period. Jesus and the New Testament writers no doubt quoted from the Old Testament (and from other sources), but it is unlikely that they knew of an authorised *book* as distinct from the concept of scriptural *books*.

## How does the Qumran sect enlarge our picture of Early Judaism?

The first thing that captures our attention about the faith of Qumran is its distinctive elements. But it is important to realise that there were many beliefs and practices that the members of the Qumran community shared with their fellow-Jews. Like other Jews, they accepted what Christians now call the Old Testament as their authoritative scriptures, believing in their divine inspiration, their historical accuracy, and the certainty that the prophecies they contained would come to pass. In line with this biblical narrative, members of the Qumran community like other Jews believed that Israel had been chosen by God to be the centre for the enactment of his purposes in the world, and that he had entered into a covenant with them that promised them blessings, material success, and triumph over their enemies if they obeyed him, but threatened them with terrible judgment if they disobeyed. Like other Jews, they thought that the measuring-rod of obedience or disobedience consisted of the degree of one's adherence to the Law of Moses, the Torah, which God had given to the people of Israel at Mount Sinai after their exodus from Egypt. This Torah was God's greatest gift to humanity, since it showed them the pathway in which they should walk in accordance with God's purpose, thus finding the fulfilment that God had intended for them. And, like many, perhaps most, other Jews, they considered some of the most important laws of the Torah to be those that related to the Temple in Jerusalem.

But these basic similarities in belief and practice should not obscure the deep alienation from and antipathy for other Jews that the people of Qumran felt. As one scholar has remarked, a Martian investigating the religious situation in Northern Ireland today might at first conclude that the Protestants and Catholics there are subdivisions of the same sociological group, since they basically believe the same things, worship the same God in the same ways, and live the same sort of life; in comparison with the overwhelmingly numerous similarities, the areas on which these two groups disagree are relatively minor (A. I. Baumgarten). This conclusion, however, would be misleading, and so would an interpretation of the Qumran community that did not recognise its sectarian nature. For, in sociological terms, the Qumran group was a sect (as, too, were the earliest Christians), that is, a group that breaks away from its parent body (in this case the Jewish community at large) and asserts in a more-or-less exclusive way that it, and it alone, is what the parent body claims to be.

Thus, for example, the members of the Qumran sect referred to their own group as 'Israel' (again a similarity to Christians). They themselves, in other words, were the true Jews, the true Israel; they were the faithful remnant of the people who had resisted the temptation to compromise and apostasize. All other people of Jewish ancestry, who had not resisted that temptation, did not really deserve to be called 'Israel.' Those outside the sect were, rather, 'children of darkness' whose apostasy from God's way would lead to their extermination in the eschatological (= endtime) war that the Qumran community believed was fast approaching.

Studying the Qumran scrolls has immeasurably enriched our knowledge about Second Temple Palestinian Judaism. Before the discovery of the scrolls, scholars knew that the Jewish community was divided into various sects from about the second century

BCE to the latter part of the first century CE. The Jewish historian Josephus mentions four sects specifically: the Pharisees, the Sadducees, the Essenes, and the 'Fourth Philosophy' of the revolutionaries. But before the discovery of the scrolls, our knowledge was disproportionately concentrated on the Pharisees, partly because they were the party that emerged victorious from the debacle of the revolt against Rome in 66-73 CE, partly because they are so important in the controversies with Jesus in the New Testament. All the other major sects, the Sadducees, the Essenes, and the 'Fourth Philosophy,' were virtually wiped out by the war, and largely for this reason we had very little information about them: they lost in the great intra-Jewish cultural battle, and subsequent history is usually not very kind to, or even very well-informed about, losers.

But now we have, in the Dead Sea Scrolls, firsthand information about a group that, if it is not identical with the Essenes, is at least related to that major sect (see above, Section 3). We now know not only how this sect was seen by positively- or negatively-inclined outsiders but also how it saw itself. We possess examples of its laws, liturgies, biblical commentaries, and prophecies of the future. The sheer creativity that is reflected in these diverse writings has helped shake up the picture that scholars drew until recently of a 'normative Judaism' spiritually and intellectually dominated by Pharisaism, in which there was not much of importance going on outside of this centre.

Another effect of the discovery of the scrolls has been to fill in our knowledge about how at least one ancient Jewish sect developed in its relation to other Jewish sects. In this regard, one of the most recently published scrolls, 'Some of the Precepts of the Law' (4QMMT) is especially revealing. What is interesting about this document, which seems to reflect a very early period in the sect's existence, is that it is so *un*sectarian. Apparently a letter from the sect's leader to the High Priest in Jerusalem, it is completely lacking in the hostility to the Jerusalem priesthood that is so prominent in later scrolls. The leader explains his opinion on various legal issues and gently expresses his hope that the High Priest will agree with him (see above, p.25). The Dead Sea sect, therefore, probably did not start out with the harsh 'us against the world' attitude that later prevailed in it. Rather, that attitude probably developed as a result of the ostracism and persecution that the sect experienced at the hands of other groups.

## What were the distinctive beliefs of the Qumran community?

### 1    Predestination

The 'Precepts of the Law' text was a surprise to many scrolls scholars because its attitude toward outsiders differed so greatly from that in the majority of the scrolls. In these other scrolls, humanity is portrayed as being divided into two eternally separate and hostile groups. On the one hand, there are the 'children of light,' the members of the Qumran community, a small enclave of holiness within the general impurity and wickedness of the world. On the other hand there are the 'children of darkness,' i.e. everyone else, including both Gentiles (= non-Jews) and apostate Jews - Jews, that is, who have not been moved to join the Qumran community.

Nor is this division merely the result of choices that members of the two groups have made on their own. Behind the children of light there stands an Angel of Light (sometimes identified with the archangel Michael), a heavenly figure who guides them in the ways of God and will eventually lead them to military victory over their human and superhuman foes. With him, and with the children of light, there stand myriads of other angels. Behind the children of darkness, on the other hand, there stands a Prince of Darkness, a Satanic figure who leads them astray and will soon manipulate them into waging an apocalyptic war against the children of light. With him, and with the children of darkness, are myriads of demonic spirits. And behind both of these heavenly 'princes,' the Prince of Darkness no less than the Angel of Light, there stands God. His is the ultimate responsibility for everything, including the wickedness of the wicked. As the beginning of the famous passage concerning the two spirits puts it:

> From the God of Knowledge comes all that is and shall be. Before ever they existed He established their whole design, and when, as he ordained them, they come into being, it is in accord with His glorious design that they accomplish their task without change. The laws of all things are in His hand and He provides them with all their needs.

> He has created man to govern the world, and has appointed for him two spirits in which to walk until the time of His visitation: the spirits of truth and injustice. Those born of truth spring from a fountain of light, but those born of injustice spring from a source of darkness. All the children of righteousness are ruled by the Prince of Light and walk in the ways of light, but all the children of injustice are ruled by the Angel of Darkness and walk in the ways of darkness.        1QS 3:15-21

The Qumran texts, then, manifest a strong belief in predestination; although human beings will be held to account for their actions, there is a sense in which they are helpless pawns of the two ruling spirits, and ultimately of God. Sectarian groups, indeed, often emphasise a belief in predestination, which offers them two great advantages in their difficult social situation: it explains the otherwise incomprehensible fact that outsiders oppose the truth of the sect (they are predestined to be blind to the light) and simultaneously emphasises the great privilege that the members of the sect possess (they are predestined to be part of the tiny group of the elect).

## 2  Eschatology (Expectations about the End)

As the above-quoted passage from 1QS indicates, this division between the two Spirits will go on only until 'the moment of His visitation,' i.e. the moment when God will intervene decisively to rectify the troubles of the world and bring in the new age of blessing, peace, and holiness. The Qumran community believed that this moment would arrive very shortly.

Indeed, there is probably a sense in which they believed that it had already begun to arrive. Already, they believed, the secrets of the new age were being revealed, including the most important secret of all: the form that the Torah would take in the Age to Come. Already God's Spirit, the active power of the new age, was at work within their community, cleansing them from impurity and setting them on the path to righteousness. Already death was, in the miraculous fellowship of the community, in a sense overcome. The Thanksgiving Hymns in particular exude gratitude for this divine outpouring of eschatological blessing:

I give you thanks, my God,
because you have done wonders with dust...
For your glory, you have purified man from sin,
so that he can make himself holy for you...
to become united with the sons of your truth
and in the lot of your holy ones,
to raise the worms of the dead
from the dust, to an [everlasting] community.

1QH 11:3, 10-12, García Martínez translation

Although it is not as pronounced as in the New Testament, therefore, a sense of 'realised eschatology' is discernible in the Dead Sea Scrolls.

But for the sectarians the new age had not yet come in its fullness. Soon it would come, but not without a terrible struggle. One of the most important Qumran texts, 'The War of the Children of Light Against the Children of Darkness' (1QM, the War Scroll), describes the course of the eschatological war the sect expected to fight very soon. It would not be a conventional war; the angels would fight on the side of the children of light (i.e. the members of the community), while the demons would fight on the side of the children of darkness (i.e. the rest of the world). Since God is incomparably stronger than any demonic power, his side would eventually win, but it would take forty years for the victory to be accomplished. Five of those forty years would be sabbatical years, in which the children of light would refrain from fighting, in accordance with the Law. The remaining thirty-five years would be divided between six years for defeating the traditional enemies of Israel and twenty-nine years for defeating other enemies. The scroll gives detailed descriptions of the order of battle, including the inscriptions on the weapons and standards of the sect's fighters. These emphasise that although the human fighters do their part in the battle, the victory is brought about by God; for example, 'On the trumpets of massacre they shall write, "The Mighty Hand of God in War shall Cause all the Ungodly Slain to Fall"' (1QM 3:8). What is envisaged, then, is a holy war like that fought by Israel in its conquest of Canaan (see further above, pp.24-25).

## 3    Anthropology (View of Human Beings)

The length of time necessary to win the eschatological holy war is testimony to the strong Qumran belief in the depth of the problem facing humanity. As already suggested, for the Qumran sectarians the problem with people is not just that they sometimes make the wrong decisions about how they should live their life, but that they are influenced or even controlled by cosmic forces of evil: demons, with Satan (usually referred to in the scrolls as 'Belial') at their head. This susceptibility to demonic control applies first and foremost to the 'children of darkness,' but Satan is also at work among the members of the elect community, and will continue to be so until this 'present evil age' gives way to the Age to Come:

> Due to the Angel of Darkness all the sons of justice stray, and all their sins, their iniquities, their failings and their mutinous deeds are under his dominion in compliance with the mysteries of God, until his [God's] moment (i.e. the moment when he intervenes decisively to defeat the Angel of Darkness)
>
> 1QS 3:20-23, García Martínez translation

Thus, being a member of the elect community does not mean that one has been permanently vaccinated against sin. Rather, the elect people of Qumran are people who experience the eschatological war in their own persons. The apocalyptic Qumran anthropology, then, is very similar to that once described by Dostoevsky: God and the Devil are fighting out a terrible battle against each other, and their battleground is the human heart. Or at least the heart of Qumran humans; outsiders are not aware of this battle, since they are totally possessed by the forces of darkness.

Because of this anthropology in which both light and darkness are present in the redeemed human, it is no surprise that the scrolls' attitude toward humanity lurches from deep pessimism to joyful exultation. In the Thanksgiving Hymns, for example, the anonymous author confesses his unworthiness in language that will remind Christian readers of the most pointed expressions of the doctrine of original sin:

... I am a creature of clay, fashioned with water, foundation of shame, source of impurity, oven of iniquity, structure of sin, spirit of mistake, astray, without knowledge, terrified by your [God's] just judgments

1QH 1:21b-23, García Martínez translation, altered

Here the human condition, which is associated with sexual intercourse ('fashioned with water') is viewed as totally sinful and alienated from God. It is a 'structure of sin.' On the basis of such passages, one scholar speaks of 'an almost pathological abhorrence of human nature' in the Thanksgiving Hymns (J Licht). Yet the author of those hymns also knows and exults in the blissful knowledge that he has been chosen by God to reveal secrets hidden from the foundation of the world. Indeed, he prefaces the above self-denigrating description with an expression of gratitude to God that 'these things I know through your knowledge, for you opened my ears to marvellous mysteries' (1QH 1:21a).

Qumran self-abnegation, therefore, is the reverse side of the sectarians' consciousness of the unmerited favour, the grace, that God had bestowed upon them. Indeed, despite the scrolls' call for intensified observance of the Law (see below), the members of the sect were under no illusions that they *deserved* the favour of God they had experienced. As a matter of fact, their concept of justification, of the basis upon which human beings can stand before God, is strikingly similar to that of Paul (and later of Luther) in its emphasis on the critical role played by the saving, undeserved, righteousness-creating power of the merciful God:

> As for me, if I stumble, the mercies of God shall be my salvation. If I stagger because of the sin of flesh, my justification shall be by the righteousness of God which endures for ever.                                                    1QS 11:11-12

## 4    The Qumran Concept of the Law

The transition from Qumran pessimism (about what human beings are naturally capable of) to Qumran optimism (about what God can enable them to do) takes place by means of the Law. It is by adherence to the Law, as it has been revealed in the Qumran community, that one is enabled by God to overcome the natural human condition of depravity, and to drink deeply of the divine goodness. Indeed, in the passage quoted above, the 'marvellous mysteries' that God has revealed are probably the mysteries of the Law. These 'mysteries' include many things that to us might seem to be matters of little spiritual significance, but that to the Qumranians and other ancient Jews were of supreme importance.

The calendar, for example. Most ancient Jews observed their holidays according to a lunar calendar - the same calendar that religious Jews still observe today, which means that each year Jewish holidays fall on a different day of our (solar) year. In contrast to other Jews, however, the Qumran sect observed a solar calendar, which means that they were 'out of synch' with their compatriots. This probably explains how, according to an important passage (1QpHab 11:4-7), the sect's enemy, the 'Wicked Priest,' could attack the sect's leader, the 'Teacher of Righteousness,' on the most holy day of the year, the Day of Atonement--a day on which no work was to be done, and on which the Wicked Priest should have been officiating at the Temple in Jerusalem. It was the Day of Atonement according to the *sect's* calendar, so they were fasting and could not defend themselves, but it was not the Day of Atonement according to the calendar of other Jews, including the Wicked Priest.

Observance of the holidays on their proper day was an important part of the Jewish Law. As noted above, the Law (Hebrew *Torah*, although the Hebrew word is probably more accurately rendered 'teaching'), was the centre of the Jewish religion. But the exact interpretation of the Law, and the method of accomplishing that interpretation, were matters of dispute. In the long run the most influential answers to these questions were those provided by the Pharisees, who developed the idea that the Law had to be interpreted in a humane way in accordance with 'the traditions of the elders', i.e. methods of interpretation that had been handed down from their predecessors and that often led to an alleviation of the severity of biblical laws. The later rabbis amplified this idea further into the concept of the Oral Law.

The Qumran sectarians would tolerate none of these innovations; they believed in observing the law in all of its rigour. Indeed, their complaint about the Pharisees was exactly the opposite of the New Testament's portrayal of them as 'laying heavy burdens' on the populace. For the Qumran group, rather, the Pharisees' problem was that they were 'seekers after smooth things', i.e. interpreters who compromised the law's severity too much; they did not lay heavy enough burdens on people! Thus, for example, the humane Pharisaic position, which was later codified in the Mishnah (*Hullin* 4:3), was that a foetus that died in its mother's womb did not render the mother ritually unclean, despite the biblical rule that contact with a corpse is defiling. For the Qumran group, however, a mother in this unfortunate situation was 'impure as a grave' until the foetus was born (11QTemple 50:11).

## 5    Purity

Purity, indeed, is a constant concern, even an obsession, at Qumran. The sectarians felt that they had been cleansed from the endemic uncleanness of the human condition by an act of divine grace; they must now safeguard their purified state by observing stringent rules of ritual cleanliness. Graphic testimony to this obsession is provided by the cisterns that dot the Qumran compound, some of them with stairs leading down to the bottom of the cistern; these cisterns, apparently, were used for the ritual bathing that played such a prominent role in the community's religious life and that symbolised cleansing from impurity by the power of the Spirit:

> He shall be cleansed from all his sins by the spirit of holiness uniting him to His [God's] truth, and his iniquity shall be expiated by the spirit of uprightness and humility. And when his flesh is sprinkled with purifying water and sanctified by cleansing water, it shall be made clean by the humble submission of his soul to all the precepts of God.

1QS 3:7-9

The understanding of ritual bathing as a cleansing by God's Holy Spirit is very close to the later Christian concept of baptism.

Purity, indeed, is so important at Qumran that the word can become a synonym for the sect itself, as in the passage in which a sinful sectarian is punished by being 'separated from the Purity' (Damascus Document 23). The reference here is in the first instance to being barred from the pure food of the sect, but the exact terminology, which suggests that the sect itself *is* 'the Purity,' is significant. As one scholar has pointed out, moreover, the importance of purity at Qumran is further illustrated by regulations that extend and intensify the biblical laws on the subject (García Martínez). Thus, for example, the Temple Scroll extends to the entire city of Jerusalem purity regulations that in the Old Testament itself apply only to the Temple. Moreover, activities that are not considered to render a person ritually unclean in the Bible or in rabbinic sources do, according to the Qumran texts, defile him. An example is defecation; the Bible does not mention it as an activity that requires subsequent ritual cleansing, and a later rabbinic source specifically declares that excrement does *not* defile the person who produces it (Jerusalem

Talmud, Pesahim 7:11); there were, moreover, lavatories in the Temple itself (Mishnah, Tamid 1:1). The Qumranians, however, apparently believed that defecation was defiling, since they stipulated that it might be done only at a considerable distance from the holy city Jerusalem (Temple Scroll 46:13-16), and they probably even prohibited it on the Sabbath, as Josephus says the Essenes did (*Jewish War* 2.147-149)!

Such regulations may seem neurotic to us, but it is important to realise that the motivation behind them is a desire to see God's sovereignty and holiness reach into every corner of human life. The Qumran folk viewed themselves as a community of priests, charged with the function of hallowing, not just the Temple, but the world. They therefore imposed upon themselves, even upon the non-priests among their members, purity regulations that in the Old Testament applied only to the priests. There is thus in the Qumran scrolls a certain counterpart to the New Testament and Reformation concept of 'the priesthood of all believers.' And the sectarians believed that this special purity, which they possessed through God's grace and their own efforts, enabled them to have fellowship with God and to be on a par with his holy angels.

## 6    Biblical Interpretation

It was mentioned above that the Qumran sectarians, like other Jewish groups, were strongly committed to the scriptures of Israel as their ultimate source of guidance and hope. Indeed, scriptural interpretation was so central to the Qumran community that it legislated that at every hour of the day or night there should be community members studying the scriptures. This legislation is itself an example of the literalistic biblical interpretation of the Qumran sect, since it is based on the description in Psalm 1 of the righteous person who meditates on God's law day and night.

The Qumran commitment to biblical interpretation led to the production of many sorts of exegetical works. The most characteristic of these is the *pesher* or commentary, a form in which a biblical book is cited passage by passage or verse by verse, and in between these citations the Qumran interpretation is

given, introduced by the word *pishro* = 'its interpretation is...'
(This form also occurs in some New Testament passages, such as
Romans 10:5-8). Besides these commentaries, the Qumran library
also includes other exegetical forms such as interpretative
paraphrases of biblical books that fill in narrative or theological
gaps, answering questions raised by the biblical text such as 'how
could Abraham, the great hero of the faith, let his wife Sarah join
Pharaoh's harem?' (Answer: God told him it was all right because
Pharaoh wouldn't touch her; Genesis Apocryphon 19-20) There
are also florilegia and testimonia, collections of biblical verses
that refer to a common theme such as the coming of the Messiah
or other eschatological events (see above, p.19).

The most important aspect of Qumran biblical interpretation
is its contemporising and eschatological character. The Qumran
sectarians, like the earliest Christians, believed that all of the
prophecies in the Old Testament were pointing to their own time.
And again like the earliest Christians, they believed that these
prophecies pointed to their own time because this time was the
beginning of the eschatological renewal. For example, in the
Qumran commentary on the Old Testament prophet Habakkuk,
we read that

> God told Habakkuk to write what was going to happen to the
> last generation, but he did not let him know the end of the age.
> And as for what he says, 'So that the one who reads it may run'
> [Habakkuk 2:2], its interpretation concerns the Teacher of
> Righteousness, to whom God has disclosed all the mysteries of
> the words of his servants, the prophets...The final age will be
> extended and go beyond all that the prophets say, because the
> mysteries of God are wonderful.

> 1QpHab 7:1-8, García Martínez translation

A complex theory of history of revelation is alluded to here, and
one that ascribes a major privilege to the exegetes of the Qumran
community. The Old Testament prophets whose words are
recorded in the Bible were, in a way, inferior to the Qumran
biblical interpreters. They were mere secretaries, taking down the

words that were dictated to them by God. But the *interpretation* of those words was hidden from them. It has now been revealed, however, to the Teacher of Righteousness, the founder of the Qumran community. At the dawn of the new age, God has brought forward an exegete to show that his ancient prophecies had been pointing to things presently taking place.

This sort of prior conviction that the ancient prophecies refer to the present day necessarily leads to a tendency to twist the ancient prophecies, since an unbiased observer would say that the original prophets were *not* talking about a time far removed from them but about their own day or a time that lay shortly in the future. In order to make the prophecies and other scriptures conform to what they want them to say, the Qumran exegetes often practised ingenious and even tortuous forms of interpretation, using variant readings, for example, or fusing scriptures with each other, or rearranging words or letters, or taking words, or parts of words, as abbreviations. These methods of forced exegesis, to be sure, were not that different from those practised by other Jews or by the early Christians, and in the Christian case as in the Qumran one the exegesis was based on the conviction that God's ultimate purposes had now been revealed with the dawning of the new age. Nor would the Qumran exegetes have admitted that they were twisting the scriptures, any more than the early Christians would have said that they were doing so. In both cases, rather, they would have said that they had been granted by God the precious interpretative key for unlocking all the mysteries of the Bible.

So authoritative did the Qumran sectarians believe that their exegesis of the Bible was, that it is sometimes difficult to tell, or to tell if *they* could tell, where the Bible left off and their own exegesis began. The sect seems to have considered its legal works, such as the Rule of the Community, the Damascus Document, and the Temple Scroll, as on a par with the legal portions of the Old Testament itself. In the Temple Scroll, moreover, biblical laws are mingled with sectarian laws, and all are indiscriminately introduced by the formula, 'He [God] said.' Thus the sectarians' enactments are regarded as just as authoritative, just as divine, just as 'revealed,' as the biblical laws.

## 7    Messianic Expectations

The Qumran sectarians, as we have seen above, believed that the scriptures pointed to their own time as the era of eschatological fulfilment. When Christians think of eschatological prophecies, they think first and foremost of the Old Testament prophecies about the coming of a Messiah - a Hebrew word that literally means 'anointed one.' In early Christianity and in rabbinic Judaism, the term 'Messiah' came to refer to a king from the lineage of David (the second king of Israel, and the founder of its dominant dynasty) who would arise at the end of days and redeem Israel. Although in the Qumran scrolls messianic expectation does not have the centrality that it does in the New Testament, the scrolls still are very important for filling in our knowledge of Jewish messianism.

The most surprising thing for Christian and Jewish readers alike is that many scrolls seem to expect not one Messiah but two. Several passages refer to 'the Messiahs of Aaron and Israel' who will come in the endtime. Aaron was the first priest of Israel, so the expected 'Messiah of Aaron' will be a priestly Messiah. The other Messiah, the 'Messiah of Israel,' is the usual kingly Messiah from David's line. It is logical that both of these eschatological figures should be referred to as 'Messiahs' (*anointed ones*), since in ancient Israel priests as well as sovereigns were anointed as a sign of their divine blessing and empowerment. Moreover, some Old Testament texts reflect the concept that the ideal for Israel is a dual leadership of a king and a High Priest, and one of them, Zechariah 4, calls these two rulers 'anointed ones'. In Jewish apocalyptic texts such as *Testament of Judah* 21:1-4, moreover, this concept of a dual kingly/priestly rule is projected into the eschatological future. What is somewhat striking is that in several Qumran passages the Messiah of Aaron = the priestly Messiah is mentioned *before* the Messiah of Israel = the Davidic Messiah.

This precedence is not accidental, since elsewhere the scrolls describe how, at the eschatological meal, the priestly Messiah will bless the food *before* the Davidic Messiah does so (1QSa 2:17-21). This precedence of the priestly Messiah over the Davidic one reflects the priestly nature of the Qumran community.

What else do the two Messiahs do, besides presiding over this eschatological meal? It is difficult to give an exact answer to this question, or even to say how important the Messiahs really were at Qumran. Some texts describe the eschatological events without invoking the Messiahs at all, or mention them only in relatively unimportant roles; in the War Scroll, for example, it is God who really wins the war for the elect, and the Davidic Messiah plays only a minor role. On the other hand, texts such as the messianic Testimonia and Florilegia concentrate a lot of attention on the Messiahs, collecting Old Testament citations and allusions to them, so they were probably important characters for the authors of those texts.

For purposes of comparison with the New Testament, moreover, it is intriguing that in one scroll (4Q246) the expected Davidic king is apparently referred to as the Son of God, an appellation that Jesus bears ubiquitously in the New Testament. Moreover, another fragmentary text (4Q521) prophesies that in the endtime heaven and earth will obey God's Messiah, a prophecy very similar to the cosmic role ascribed to Jesus in passages such as Matthew 28:18-20 and Philippians 2:9-11. This passage also describes how at the eschaton either God or the Messiah will 'heal the sick, raise the dead, and preach good news to the poor' - a description strikingly reminiscent of the New Testament's characterisation of the mission of Jesus the Messiah (Matthew 11:5 parallel Luke 7:22; the Matthean/Lukan parallel reflects their use of a common source of sayings of Jesus, which scholars designate 'Q'). Both the Qumran passage and the Gospels passages allude to Isaiah 61:1, in which God's spirit anoints a messenger to preach good news to the poor. But both go beyond Isaiah 61, and in exactly the same way, in speaking of this messenger raising the dead. It seems probable, therefore, that either Jesus himself or the Q source knew and utilised the Qumran elaboration of Isaiah 61 that is enshrined in 4Q521.

In addition to their expectation of two Messiahs, the Qumran sectarians seem also to have expected a third eschatological figure, a prophet. 1QS 9:11 says that the sect's first edition of the Law will remain in force 'until the prophet comes, and the Messiahs of Aaron and Israel.' This prophetic expectation probably reflects an Old Testament passage, Deuteronomy 18:15-18, in which Moses predicts that after his death God will raise up for Israel 'a prophet like me,' to whom they must listen or suffer the covenant curses. Although the original Deuteronomy passage probably refers to a succession of Mosaic prophets and was not eschatological, it was interpreted at Qumran as a prophecy of the advent of a single eschatological figure, *the* Prophet-like-Moses. It is unclear exactly what the members of the Qumran sect thought this Prophet would do, though he may be identical to 'the Interpreter of the Law' referred to in CD 6:8; this makes sense, because Moses was Israel's first and most important lawgiver. In any case, the Qumran expectations about 'the Prophet' seem to have been part of a more general Jewish hope for a Mosaic Prophet, which sometimes coalesced with the hope for a Messiah figure and is reflected in the New Testament as well as in other places. In John 1:21, 25, for example, John the Baptist is questioned about whether he is the Messiah, or Elijah, or 'the Prophet,' and in Acts 3:17-26 the Deuteronomic Prophet-like-Moses passage is interpreted as a reference to Jesus.

## 8    New Temples

As just mentioned, the scrolls' greater concentration on the Priestly Messiah than on the Davidic Messiah reflects the priestly nature of the Qumran community. This priestly character in turn reflects the history of the community, which seems to have originally been formed by priests who broke away from the Jerusalem establishment because they considered that establishment to be corrupt and to have polluted the Temple by their corruption.

Priests, however, need a Temple; without it they lack a *raison d'être*. So the priestly community reacted to their 'loss' of the Temple by constructing three images to replace it:

1    They dreamed of a restoration of the Temple that would re-establish it as a place of true worship; this restoration would involve, among other things, the reinstatement of a proper priesthood and the imposition of rigorous standards of purity. This is the restored earthly Temple that is described in great detail in the Qumran Temple Scroll (see above, pp.15-16).

2    This restored earthly Temple, however, is apparently different from *another* Temple to whose establishment the Qumran sectarians looked forward, a sanctuary which God himself would create at the eschaton. The two future Temples are distinguished in 11QTemple 29:8-10:

I [God] will dwell with them for ever and ever and will sanctify my [sa]nctuary [= the restored earthly Temple] by my glory. I will cause my glory to rest on it until the day of creation on which I shall create my sanctuary [= the new, heavenly Temple], establishing it for myself for all time according to the covenant which I have made with Jacob in Bethel'

cf. Genesis 28:10-22; 35:1-15; Vermes translation, altered

The two sanctuaries are both future ('I *will* dwell with them...I *shall* create my sanctuary'), but they are separate from each other; the first will exist *'until* the day of [new] creation' upon which God will create the second. Only the second, then, is properly eschatological.

Yet there are difficulties with the distinction between two future Temples. It is hard, for example, to see how the sectarians could have expected the earthly Temple to be restored before the end of the present evil age. Moreover, it may be wondered whether the two-Temple scheme is rigidly followed in other Qumran documents; which of the future Temples, for example, is being described in 4QFlorilegium 1:1-7, which speaks of a sanctuary that God will build in the last days, from which foreigners and unclean persons will be excluded? This sounds like an eschatological Temple, yet the list of excluded persons is reminiscent of parts of the Temple Scroll that describe the restored earthly Temple. It may be that we should not expect too much consistency from the Qumran descriptions.

3     But the community also apparently thought that, even before the erection of these physical Temples, a true Temple already existed that was unaffected by the corruption of the Jerusalem authorities. This was the Temple of the community, in which true, spiritual sacrifices were already being offered. In 4QFlorilegium 1:6-7, for example, we hear of God's command 'that a Sanctuary of humanity be built for Himself, that there they may send up, like the smoke of incense, the works of the Law' (Vermes translation, altered; cf. also 1QS 9:3-5). This idea of the community as God's Temple also has New Testament parallels.

In many ways, then, the Qumran sectarians inhabited a religious universe that was an alternative to, or more precisely a replacement of, the religious universe in which other Jews lived. The present physical Temple might be barred to them because of its corruption in their eyes, but they worshipped in a spiritual Temple that had taken the place of that centre of apostasy and that foreshadowed the restored physical Temple and the heavenly sanctuary of the new age. They might be viewed by other Jews as a marginal group, but in their own eyes they were the true Israel who preserved within their community the genuine form of the Law and the proper way of interpreting the rest of the Scriptures. They were, in short, what the rest of Israel claimed to be, but was not. As one scholar has put it, then, the Qumran self-understanding was the first example in Jewish history of a theology of substitution (S Talmon). The early Christian self-understanding was the second.

# 5 THE SIGNIFICANCE OF THE DEAD SEA SCROLLS FOR UNDERSTANDING EARLY CHRISTIANITY

## Is Jesus mentioned in the scrolls?

No. There is no known *express* reference to Jesus of Nazareth in the scrolls.

So much can be said without fear of contradiction. Nor is it very surprising, for two reasons. In the first place, the majority of the scrolls were written before the turn of the era, so are unlikely to have referred to someone as yet not born. In the second, the Qumran scrolls tend not to refer to people expressly by their names. More usually what we get is a more colourful type-casting: 'the Spouter of Lies', 'the Wicked Priest', 'the Teacher of Righteousness', more reminiscent of Gotham City than of sober history books.

But this lack of direct naming of personages in the Qumran literature brings its own problems. Might not one of these terms actually be a coded, cryptic reference to Jesus? There are two difficulties here: how to prove (or at least to make out a decent case for saying) that Jesus was meant by one of these terms; and how to disprove any such claims that might be made. For some, such difficulties are an invitation to make bold, unsubstantiated, but equally not easily disprovable claims. Barbara Thiering has for instance suggested that 'the Wicked Priest' refers to Jesus; R Eisenman takes 'the Teacher of Righteousness' to refer to James the brother of Jesus. (See further, below.)

How likely is it that 'the Wicked Priest' refers to Jesus? One would think that any responsible attempt to decode such terms would have to be developed along the following lines. First, one would need to define, as far as possible, the period of history to which the texts were referring. One would then have to assemble the statements about 'the Wicked Priest' in the various scrolls which mention this figure. Finally, one would attempt to make an identification between 'the Wicked Priest' and some known historical figure in the period indicated. All this seems obvious enough and is for instance the procedure followed by G Vermes in his introduction to his translation of the scrolls.

The clearest indication of dating for these characters is given in the opening of the Damascus Document. Here we read that 'at the moment of wrath, three hundred and ninety years after having delivered them up into the hands of Nebuchadnezzar, king of Babylon,' God caused 'to sprout from Israel and Aaron a shoot of the planting, in order to possess the land'. This dates these events to somewhere at the beginning of the second century BCE. Nebuchadnezzar conquered Jerusalem in 586. 390 years later would be 196, but we should not press ancient datings too hard. It would make more sense to identify the 'moment of wrath' with the attack on Judaism under Antiochus Epiphanes (175-164 BCE). This would further suggest that the 'shoot of the planting' should be identified with the group of 'the Hasidaeans, mighty warriors of Israel, everyone of whom offered himself willingly for the Law', mentioned in 1 Maccabees 2:42. The Damascus Document goes on to say that this group of devout followers at first 'were like blind persons and like those who grope for the path over twenty years' and that then God gave them the Teacher of Righteousness to 'direct them in the path of his heart'. This is also the time at which 'the Scoffer arose, who scattered the water of lies over Israel'. Vermes argues that we should identify the Scoffer with the Wicked Priest mentioned in 1QpHab 8:8-9, who was first known by the name of truth, and therefore by implication later become a liar. Of him we also learn that he and his followers were 'traitors to the community' (2:1), that he then 'ruled over Israel' (8:10), 'stole and hoarded wealth from the brutal men who had rebelled against God' (8:11), that 'he pursued the Teacher of

Righteousness' (11:5), that he 'performed repulsive acts and defiled the Sanctuary of God' (12:8-9). All of this seems to point to a painful and violent rift within the original resistance group of devotees of the Law. It looks as if the Wicked Priest was one of the Jewish leaders who assumed the High Priesthood after Antiochus Epiphanes had been successfully driven off.

How then might one identify the Wicked Priest with Jesus? Only by locating the texts in a much later period. Then one may identify the Teacher of Righteousness with John the Baptist and Jesus with the one who was formerly a disciple of John but then left together with some of John's disciples to start his own ministry, and whose actions in the Temple could be construed as its defilement. The problem with this view is not only that it makes the texts refer to a period much later than that indicated by the passage in the Damascus Document 1 but also that it leads those who follow it to set John and Jesus within a nationalistic and militant strand of Judaism, which seems strangely at odds with the New Testament records.

## Was John the Baptist associated with Qumran?

There are clearly a number of points of contact between John and Qumran. There is first a matter of geographical proximity: John is associated with the wilderness. He is said to have received his call in the wilderness (Luke 3:2). He baptized in the Jordan which flows into the north of the Dead Sea. The precise location of John's activity (John 3:23: at Aenon near Salim) is not known for sure, but it must have been within walking distance of Qumran. It is hardly thinkable that John would not have been aware of (i.e. have known a good deal about) what went on there. On the other hand, Qumran was not the only religious movement or site in the desert. Josephus (*Life* 11-12) tells us that he spent time in the desert with Bannus, a figure whose clothing and food was similar to that of John. Did John have closer contact with Qumran?

Luke (1:5-25) tells us that John's father, Zecharia, was an elderly priest who did duty in the Temple. It is not unthinkable that if John was orphaned at an early age he should have been brought up by the community at Qumran or by some other group of Essenes. (Josephus, *Jewish War* 2.120 tells us that the Essenes adopted others' children). However there are too many problems about this to put much weight on it. Luke's account is full of legendary motifs; and the Temple priesthood and the Qumran community were antagonistic towards one another.

Much more impressive are the connections between John's message and actions and those of Qumran. John goes out into the desert to 'prepare the way of the Lord' (Matthew 3:3; Mark 1:2; Luke 3:4 citing Isaiah 40:3). Qumran uses the same text to refer to the work of the community in establishing a community which lives according to the Law and which will atone for the earth (1QS 8:14). John baptizes with water in the Jordan. The Qumran community had regular daily washings. John called people out into the desert to repent of their sins and be baptized against the coming judgment (Matthew 3:5-6; Mark 1:4; Luke 3:3). Josephus indicates that 'righteousness towards one's fellows and piety towards God' was a necessary condition of John's baptism which was 'a purification of the body' (*Antiquities* 18:117). Qumran enjoins its initiates to adhere to the teachings of the community, to hate all that is opposed to it and only allows them to enter the waters of the community when they have been through a considerable period of testing. Then daily lustrations mark the determination of the members to eschew the ways of darkness from which they have separated (1QS). Both John and Qumran live in lively anticipation of a final judgment when God will reward the righteous and destroy the wicked (Matthew 3:16-12; Luke 3:9; 1QS 4:6-14). John expects a 'stronger one' who will bring judgment and renewal in the Spirit. Qumran looks to the coming of Davidic and Aaronic Messiahs (see above pp.74-76).

All these points of contact show that John and Qumran inhabit the same world of apocalyptic expectation: they have a similar sense of the radical perversion of the present world and of the need for Israel to repent. They have similar rites which mark the division of their followers from the sin and darkness of the present age. They expect a final act of divine intervention which will restore God's rule to the world and which will be ushered in by divine agent(s). Do they show that John was a product of Qumran? Or were such ideas in more general circulation?

Certainly such ideas were in wider circulation and the apocalyptic literature which is found in Qumran (e.g. 1 Enoch) shows that Qumran itself was aware of the existence of such ideas in other books. More generally, apocalyptic movements like those of Qumran and John have their roots not only in widely circulating ideas but in social, economic and political conditions which lead people to seek relief in visions of some final overthrow of their enemies and vindication for their own group. Moreover, there are significant differences between Qumran and John. Qumran is an apocalyptic movement with a history. The original call to go out into the desert was issued, we must suppose, in the second century BCE. The community which was now established in the desert was one certainly with expectations but which had nevertheless lived through its initial period of excited expectation of the end. For John the sense of urgency was much greater: 'The axe is already laid to the roots of the tree' (Matthew 3:10). Those who were baptized by John had to bear fruits of repentance: to go back and lead a simple life of justice in anticipation of the imminent end. No time here for elaborate periods of initiation and testing. By contrast those who entered the community at Qumran were entering a community with a tight structure and were, arguably at least, more concerned with understanding the times, trying to set the history of their community within some apocalyptic time frame.

This is to emphasise the significantly different mood of Qumran and John. John is borne along by a spirit of apocalyptic enthusiasm which is very different from Qumran's concern for the orderly regulation of its community and its distinction from those who it sees as living in darkness. Of course it does not mean that John could not have emerged from such a community. There is no law which says that people from such communities may not be caught up by apocalyptic visions of a more dramatic and urgent kind, such as that of John. So it remains an open question whether John was ever a member of the community. The closeness of John's baptism to the lustrations at Qumran might suggest that John had some familiarity with their customs; it cannot prove that John ever spent long periods at Qumran.

## Was Jesus an Essene/Qumran member?

There is no reason to link Jesus with the Qumran community. Key elements of Jesus' teaching and behaviour stress the need for openness to those outside the Jewish community: Jesus teaches love of enemies (Matthew 5:43-48); he shares meals with tax-collectors and sinners (Mark 2:15-17); he is recorded as having broken with Jewish purity regulations (Mark 7:14-19). This contrasts sharply with Qumran's emphasis on love of the brotherhood and rejection of those outside; with its willingness to allow people to share their meals only after a long period of probation as members of the community; and with the great emphasis on observation of purity regulations in the life of the community by the Dead Sea.

Even if one makes a link between John and Qumran, this does not mean that this link carries over to Jesus. Many came to John and not all of them could have had prior links with Qumran. Whatever the link between John and Qumran, his own ministry and vivid expectation of coming judgment marks a move away from Qumran; Jesus' ministry was seen by his contemporaries as sharply contrasting with the ascetic style of John: 'For John came neither eating nor drinking, and they say, "He has a demon"; the Son of Man came eating and drinking, and they say, "Behold, a glutton and a drunkard, a friend of tax collectors and sinners!" Yet wisdom is justified by her deeds.' (Matthew 11:18-19)

## Are the Dead Sea Scrolls, the Essenes or Qumran mentioned in the New Testament?

There is certainly no mention of Qumran or indeed of any community on the Dead Sea in the New Testament. Moreover, although we hear of other contemporary Jewish groups and figures (the Pharisees, Sadducees, Samaritans and John the Baptist, Theudas and Judas the Galilean - leaders of contemporary insurrections), we do not have any mention of the Essenes.

This is certainly surprising The Essenes are mentioned more than once in contemporary Jewish and non-Jewish literature (Philo, Pliny, Josephus) which suggests that they were well known and influential. On the other hand the term Essene (*Essenoi* or *Essaioi* in Greek, *Esseni* in Latin) probably goes back to an Aramaic *chasaia*, meaning the pious ones, which nowhere occurs in the Qumran texts (see above pp.34-39). If the Qumran texts do not refer to the term, it is perhaps not so surprising that the New Testament does not either.

The New Testament contains no known quotations of the scrolls written by the Qumran community. There may however be indirect references to the scrolls, as opposed to similarities of ideas and beliefs which we shall discuss below. The distinction is rather fine, but one example may suffice. Jesus in Matthew 5:43 says: 'You have heard that it was said, "You shall love your neighbour and hate your enemy".' This reference to 'hating your enemy' might be a polemical echo of sayings like that in 1QS 1:10-11: 'to love all the sons of light, each one according to his lot in God's plan, and to detest all the sons of darkness, each one in accordance with his blame in God's vindication.' However scholars are by no means agreed whether Jesus's remark is a direct attack on Qumran or a more general clarification of the meaning of the Levitical command to love one's neighbour.

### Do the Dead Sea Scrolls contain Christian documents?

There are no generally acknowledged Christian documents among the scrolls but recently a Spanish scholar, José O'Callaghan, has argued that one of the fragments found in Cave 7 at Qumran is a fragment of Mark's Gospel, containing parts of Mark 6:52-3.

Cave 7 contains only fragments in Greek. By general agreement, the only one of these fragments where a serious case can be mounted for identification with the New Testament is 7Q5; any other identifications would depend on the prior identification of this one. The fragment is only five lines long and consists of a few letters in each line. Moreover, these are not easy to read and scholars differ in their readings.

Much of the dispute centres on the reading of one, only half-legible, letter. O'Callaghan and his followers (including Carsten Thiede) read the letter as a Greek N (Nu), others as an I (Iota) and A (Alpha). If the latter reading is accepted this fragment cannot be related to Mark 6. If the former, it may be - but may also be a fragment of some other text: recently an alternative source has been suggested, from the Greek text of Enoch. (For a full discussion of this matter, see O Betz and R Riesner, *Jesus, Qumran and the Vatican*, London: SCM Press, 1994, pp.114-24). The matter is clearly not yet fully resolved, but the burden of proof remains with those who argue for the Markan identification.

## Were some early Christians Essenes?

Precisely because of the lack of specific reference to Qumran or the Essenes in the New Testament it is impossible to say for certain whether any Christians belonged to the Essenes. It is of course quite possible that some Christians had originally been Essenes: Essenes and Christians shared a broadly similar eschatological outlook. Like the Christians, they were 'looking for the kingdom of God' (Mark 15:43). If John the Baptist had originally been a member of the community at Qumran, then this would strengthen the possibility: certainly there is evidence that some of John's disciples became disciples of Jesus (John 1:35-39). Evidence (see below) for similarities of organisational structure and thought between the early Christian communities and Qumran might suggest that there was movement of members between the two groups. All of this however falls far short of proof that Christians were actually Essenes at the same time as they were active members of the Christian church.

Nevertheless there are those who have suggested that there were Christians who indeed had prominent positions within the

Qumran community. Among these, R Eisenman has claimed that James the brother of Jesus is to be identified as the Teacher of Righteousness, suggesting that both Jesus and James belonged to a nationalistic strain of Judaism which was represented at Qumran. The real problem with this view is the same as that raised in discussing Barbara Thiering's identification of Jesus and the Wicked Priest. Archaeological and palaeographical evidence (analysis of the scribes' handwriting), as well as radiocarbon dating, place the majority of the scrolls before the turn of the era (see above pp.4-5); the internal evidence of the scrolls, notably the suggested dating for the origins of the community in the Damascus Document, confirms this and suggests a date for the events in which the Teacher of Righteousness and the Wicked Priest were involved sometime in the second century BCE (see above pp.80-81). All of this means that speculations about an identification between James the brother of Jesus and the Teacher of Righteousness are no more than that: and baseless ones at that.

## What are the main similarities between the organisation of the Qumran sect and the early churches?

There are a number of points at which comparison can be made between the organisation of the Qumran sect and at least some of the early Christian communities. The Christian communities were quite diverse, so one should expect that not all points of comparison will hold across all of them.

1    The central rites of Qumran and early Christianity bear striking resemblance. Admission to the community at Qumran was through entering into the covenant by an oath. After a further period of probation the initiand was admitted to the waters of purification and to the common meal ('the pure food, [literally, "purity"], of the men of holiness', 1QS 5:7-20). Those who subsequently were in breach of the community's regulations might be punished by exclusion from the meals and the daily lustrations. Clearly there are striking resemblances here between the waters of purification and Christian baptism (which is also linked to a public confession of sins and of faith) and between the

community's meal and the Christian Eucharist. Rituals of washing/immersion and a community meal are in both cases the defining rites of the two groups.

2    In both communities the assembly of the adherents played a central role in the regulation of community affairs and in matters of doctrine.  In Qumran there appears to have been a council (of 12 men and 3 priests) set over the community which was the ultimate authority in matters of discipline and doctrine; in the smaller communities of Essenes the congregation itself would decide matters, though even here there would be some kind of overseer.  Early Christian communities regulated their affairs in quite diverse ways, yet we can see the same tendency to give an important role to the congregation as well as recognising certain supervisory roles allotted to specific individuals (apostles, prophets and teachers, 1 Corinthians 12:28-29; Ephesians 4:11, cf. Acts 13:1; Ephesians 3:5; Revelation 18:20).  In Matthew 18:15-18 we find a very similar account of disciplinary procedures to that in 1QS 5:24-6:1.  In both cases, if there is a dispute between members they should first attempt to resolve it on their own. If this fails, then they should discuss the matter in front of witnesses; finally, they may bring the matter to the congregation.  Early Christians met together to attempt to resolve doctrinal disputes. In Acts 15 we hear of an assembly (Greek *plethos*, 'multitude', cf. Qumran's Hebrew: *rabim*, 'many') of the apostles and elders which listened to the arguments of both sides over the question of the admission of the Gentiles. The final judgment is one which commended itself to 'the apostles and elders, with the whole church' (15:22).

3    The community in Qumran held its property in common. Those who entered the community transferred their possessions into the community's treasury after a period of testing (1QS 6:18-23).  The early Christian community in Jerusalem held its goods in common and distributed to 'each as any had need' (Acts 2:44-45; 4:32-37; 5:1-11).  Similar policies of mutual support and pooling of resources may have operated in some at least of Paul's

churches. Paul also expended considerable energy on taking up a collection for the poor in Jerusalem, cf: Galatians 2:10; 2 Corinthians 8 & 9; Romans 15:25-33.

## What are the main differences in organisation between Qumran and the early churches?

1    There are obvious differences between the lustrations at Qumran and the Christian practice of baptism. Christian baptism is a once-only act of initiation, whereas Qumran lustrations are not strictly initiation rituals at all. Initiation at Qumran is focused on the ceremony of entering the covenant (see 1QS 1:16-2:18); only after a subsequent and extended period of testing does the initiand gain access to the waters of purification and take part in the daily rites of purification. Participation in the ritual washings of the community is a mark of sustained membership, not an admission rite as such. For Christians, on the other hand, baptism marks the point of entry into the community: they die to the old life and are taken into a new way of life by conformity to Christ's death (so at least Paul: Romans 6:3-11).

For Qumran the lustrations are principally a means of purifying the members of the congregation. Although they are ruled over by the Spirit of Light, they are subject to pollution by the actions of the Spirit of Darkness, who 'leads all the children of righteousness astray' (1QS 3:22); for Christians baptism is a mark or a means of their incorporation into the fellowship of the church and of the gift of the Spirit: 'For by one Spirit we were all baptized into one body - Jews or Greeks, slaves or free - and all were made to drink of one Spirit.' (1 Corinthians 12:13)

2    For both Qumran and the early Christians some form of common meal was a central mark of their fellowship. The differences here are more ones of style and theological symbolism. According to Josephus (*Jewish War* 2.129-133), the meals of the Essenes were highly disciplined and orderly affairs. After washing they entered the refectory, 'as though into a holy precinct'; the baker and the cook served out the food: 'only one bowlful of each dish to each man', and then grace was said. Their

meals were marked by their orderliness and 'their invariable sobriety'. By contrast, it was a matter of grief to Paul that the meals of the early Christian communities were disorderly and that the distribution of food was unequal: 'For in eating, each one goes ahead with his own meal, and one is hungry and another is drunk' (1 Corinthians 11:21). This contrast is stark and in a sense a product of the very different forms of symbolisation which the meals of the two communities represent. The orderly meals at Qumran represent the need for close discipline within their communities: at all times they need to be on their guard against the Angel of Darkness who causes the sons of light to stray (1QS 3:21-25). The community needs a rigorously structured hierarchy to ensure that it preserves from error the understanding of the Law entrusted to it. Thus at meals members sit according to their rank and contact with a junior can cause pollution, necessitating washing (Josephus, *Jewish War* 2.150: 'they wash themselves as though they had been in contact with a stranger'). By contrast, at Christian meals, those who are present find their unity in the Spirit, a much more unpredictable and uncontrollable sort of phenomenon. Nor is it clear that these meals were restricted to believers. 1 Corinthians 14:23 obviously envisages outsiders coming into the Christian assembly. Jesus' meals with tax-collectors and sinners must have provided some kind of a precedent for those familiar with such stories, though we cannot easily know how this will have developed. Nevertheless for Paul, clearly angry at the disorder, the answer is not tighter discipline, but purer spirituality: they are to examine themselves and make sure that when they eat and drink they recall Jesus' death and their expectation of his coming again. The meal is becoming less of a community feast, more of a religious act of commemoration and spiritual renewal.

3    While there are, as we have seen, considerable similarities between the management of community discipline and teaching at Qumran and in the early Christian communities, this should not lead us to overlook the differences. The most striking differences in this respect relate to i) the presence within Qumran of

*institutions for determining rank and seniority* (e.g. the Renewal of the Covenant ceremony where members were re-graded, 1QS 2:19-25; 5:24), and ii) the use of *accepted and formulated codes of discipline* (1QS 6:24-7:25). This is not at all surprising, given Qumran's much longer history and geographical isolation and cohesion. Living together for a long time on the same spot provides ample opportunity for developing standardised methods of dealing with community strains and conflict. By contrast, the Christian communities of the New Testament period were young, widely dispersed and subject to the attentions of a mixture of visiting prophets and teachers with varying views and beliefs. It would take at least another century before the churches began to approach the same levels of structural differentiation and ideological definition that we find in Qumran.

4      Again there is no denying the close similarities between Qumran's and some early Christian groups' pooling and sharing of resources. These are striking not least because they stand out in the ancient world and, in the case of the Essenes, were clearly seen by commentators like Josephus as unusual and exemplary. However there is a greater diversity of approach to these questions within Christianity. Jesus gives rather different directions about wealth and property in the Gospels: Matthew 19:21; Luke 19:8-10; cf. Matthew 26:11. Within the Pauline churches the dominant model of mutual support is often thought to have been the house church where the community gathered under the patronage of a wealthy member, a kind of 'love-patriarchalism'. The dominance of this model may however have been overstressed by scholars; Christians living in the crowded tenements of cities like Thessalonica and Rome may have adopted a life-style more like that of the Essenes, sharing what they had, relying on those who could work to earn a living to support those who could not. The passage in  2 Thessalonians 3:6-13, with its injunction: 'If any one will not work, let him not eat', may reflect the need to encourage all those who could work to do so for the good of the whole community.

**What aspects of the theology of the Dead Sea Scrolls shed light on the New Testament and early Christianity?**

One of the great benefits of the Dead Sea Scrolls for New Testament scholars is the fact that they give evidence of Jewish beliefs and practices contemporary with early Christianity. Clearly Qumran was in many senses a marginalised community and it should therefore not be thought necessarily representative of first century Judaism as a whole. On the other hand, it does clearly preserve Jewish language and thought of the period and this is of the greatest value for understanding the meaning of the New Testament documents and for setting them in a wider context of belief and practice. The following list of topics is by no means exhaustive but points to important areas where the scrolls can illuminate matters of relevance to the New Testament.

1    Eschatology and Messianism

Like many first century Jews, the community at Qumran entertained hopes and fears about the future when God would set his world to rights and vindicate his people or at least, and this is particularly true of Qumran, the remnant that had been faithful to him. In 1QS 4:16-14 we read of the 'visitation' of those who have walked respectively in the Spirits of Light and Darkness. The sons of light will receive 'healing, great peace in a long life and fruitfulness, together with every everlasting blessing and eternal joy in life without end, a crown of glory and a garment of majesty in unending light', a splendid mixture of this-worldly and eternal rewards. The sons of darkness by contrast will have the worst of both worlds: 'a multitude of plagues by the hand of all the destroying angels, everlasting damnation by the avenging wrath of the fury of God, eternal torment and endless disgrace together with shameful extinction in the fire of the dark regions.' Logic may lose out to emotion when it comes to contemplating the fate of one's enemies: they will enjoy eternal torment *and* everlasting extinction. Such ideas are not without precedent in the Jewish literature of the time; they find some reflection in the New Testament (Matthew 8:12; 22:13; 25:30; 2 Peter 2:4 and

Revelation) and have enjoyed considerable popularity in subsequent Christian thought and art.

Qumran also looked forward in the War Scroll to a final battle in which their enemies, more closely identified with Romans (the Kittim), would be overthrown after a long struggle by the direct intervention of God (1QM 18:1). This was a grandiose vision of world dominion for a small closed community. Such views are quite widespread in the Jewish literature of the time. The forces of evil, inspired and led by Satanic powers, will be engaged in a last battle with the forces of light, led by Michael and his angels. Only after such a period of affliction and cosmic upheaval will the world finally be purged of evil and the reign of peace and justice begin.

These views find their reflection in different ways in the New Testament. The fullest and most dramatic account of such cosmic warfare is in Revelation 12-14, where God's angels bring judgment and wrath on those who have been rebellious. 'Now war arose in heaven, Michael and his angels fighting against the dragon; and the dragon and his angels fought, but there was no longer any place for them in heaven. And the great dragon was thrown down, that ancient serpent, who is called Devil and Satan, the deceiver of the whole world' (12:7-9). In the ensuing mythical narrative a great beast arises from the sea to make war on the saints. For a time it has authority over all nations and everyone worships it. Ranged against the beast and his followers is 'the Lamb with the hundred and forty-four thousand who had his name and his Father's name written on their forehead' (14:1). It is these who will escape the coming wrath when the reaper angels fly out to execute judgment on the followers of Satan.

Revelation's dramatic mythology is not the only way that these themes are played out in the New Testament. In Mark 13 we read that there will be wars and persecution before the end, when the Son of Man will appear to gather in the elect from the four corners of the earth. Before this time, the disciples will have preached the Gospel to all nations (13:10). There are also passages which suggest that the end has in some sense already come with the arrival of Jesus. In Matthew 9:38 Jesus, seeing the harassed and helpless crowds, says 'Pray therefore the Lord of the harvest to send out labourers into his harvest.'

One clear mark of this sense that the end has already arrived is the widespread tendency in the New Testament to identify Jesus with the Messiah (see above pp.74-76 for a discussion of the Messianic figures in the Scrolls). The title 'Christ' becomes little more than part of Jesus' name, 'Jesus Christ'. Christian belief in Jesus as the Messiah is reflected in certain titles, notably 'Son of David' and the direct confession of him as the Christ, most famously in Peter's confession in Mark 8:29. It is however clear that Jesus' life and death are not what would have been expected of a Davidic Messiah, who was anticipated as the one who would overcome Israel's enemies and establish God's rule. Jesus, by contrast, meets his death at the hands of the occupying Roman soldiers. Do such views find any echo in Qumran?

The answer is again, almost certainly, no. The hesitation derives from the fact that claims have been made, variously by John Allegro and R H Eisenman that one fragment from cave 4 (4Q285) contains a reference to the killing of the Messiah. This is odd because the passage is based on Isaiah 11, which is elsewhere (1Q28b) interpreted of the prince of the community who is victorious over his enemies. Eisenman translated the relevant line: 'they shall put to death the leader of the community' but the Hebrew may also be translated 'the leader of the community will put him to death' (see above, p.25).

## 2    The Spirit, divine omnipotence and predestination

Qumran has a striking doctrine of the Spirit which is found in its most fully developed form in 1QS 3-4. Here God is said to assign two spirits to 'man', by which he is to walk, the Angel of Darkness and the Prince of Light. They rule over two distinct groupings, the sons of light and darkness, and govern their thoughts and their actions. Moreover the Spirit of Darkness attempts to subvert the sons of light and to lead them astray (1QS 3:15-26).

This is similar to the doctrine found in the Book of Jubilees (an extra-biblical text found in the Qumran library) which (ch.15) tells how God has set different spirits over the nations, while he himself rules over Israel. Such doctrines are a massive assertion of the sovereignty of God: *everything*, no matter how repulsive, and indeed how contrary to his will, is ultimately to be attributed to him: 'From the God of knowledge stems all there is and all there shall be. Before they existed he made all their plans and when they shall come into being they will execute all their works in compliance with his instructions, according to his glorious design without altering anything' (1QS 3:15-16).

One of the interesting things about this kind of spirituality is that it does not, as one might think, produce zombies who think of themselves as having no choice or control over their own actions. On the contrary, it is linked to strong moral exhortation and considerable moral sensibility. In the passage on the two Spirits, there is a long exposition of the two ways in which those ruled over by the two Spirits walk: 'it is a spirit of meekness, of patience, generous compassion, eternal goodness, intelligence, understanding, potent wisdom which trusts in all the deeds of God and depends on his abundant mercy' (1QS 4:3-4).

The similarities with the New Testament are not far to seek. Paul has a similarly strong doctrine of the Spirit which inspires the church and produces in it different 'charisms', gifts (1 Cor 12; Rom 12:3-8, where God has apportioned a different measure of faith to each member of the church) which furthermore are coordinated by the Spirit in such a way that diversity does not (should not?) lead to disunity. In Galatians 5 he speaks about the fruit of the Spirit in terms similar to 1QS 4:3-4. Paul even occasionally strays into the language of double predestination, comparing those accepting of and opposed to God's will to different kinds of pots made by a divine potter: vessels of mercy and vessels of wrath (Romans 9:19-24). On the other hand, when he speaks of the fruit of the Spirit, these are contrasted with the works of the flesh and there is no suggestion that this is appointed by God or indeed that those who walk according to the flesh cannot receive the Spirit and walk in newness of life. Life in the Spirit is a life of freedom from bondage to sin, the flesh and 'beggarly spirits'.

## 3    Covenant and election

Along with these doctrines of the Spirit and predestination went a strong emphasis on covenant and election. Those who entered the community at Qumran swore an oath and thereby entered the covenant community and undertook to obey all the commandments of God. There was an annual ceremony when the covenant vows were renewed and the members of the community were ranked in accordance with their understanding and performance of the Law as interpreted by the community. The hymns of the community make clear that those in the community saw their membership as the result of divine guidance and election: 'these are those you [God] founded before the centuries ... so that they can recount your glory throughout all your kingdom' (1QH 5:13-17). Again we find the combination of a strong doctrine of divine sovereignty and an equally strong emphasis on the need for obedience to his will. The notion of God having made a covenant with his people has strong biblical associations. The use here is unusual in that there is no explicit link with Jewish ancestry or indeed reference to circumcision, which is seen as a mark of this covenant. The absence of such references does not mean that these matters were neglected. They would be understood.    But the fact that the community distinguished itself sharply from all other people, *Jews included*, would have meant that descent from Abraham and circumcision would no longer serve as identity markers for the community. Instead taking the oath of the covenant as administered by the community became the distinctive mark of these Jews.

Emphasis on covenant is nothing like so marked in the New Testament. It does occur in relation to the Last Supper, both in the accounts of Jesus' 'words of institution' in the Gospels and in Paul's discussion of it in 1 Corinthians 11:25. Paul also refers to the new faith as a new covenant by contrast with the old, in 2 Corinthians 3. The writer of the Epistle to the Hebrews speaks of Jesus as the mediator of the new covenant (9:15), by which 'those who are called may receive the promise of an eternal inheritance'. But again there are differences in emphasis and interpretation. Paul tends to make the contrast between the old and the new covenant in terms of Law. The old covenant depends upon a written code, the new is 'in the Spirit' (2 Corinthians 3:6). The Qumran oath obliged initiands to do all the works of the Law; for Paul initiation into the church meant walking in the Spirit. Thus although Christianity, like Qumran, was a religion based not on ethnicity but on an individual's own choice, it did not make a solemn covenant oath and commitment to do the Law its primary identity marker. Its central initiation rite stressed incorporation into a new community in the Spirit and in union with Christ.

Election certainly plays a role in the New Testament writings. Paul sees his own role as apostle to the Gentiles as one that has been foreordained (Galatians 1:15). Christians were 'called saints', holy ones, singled out by God's call. This new calling was something that transcended (in principle at least) all ethnic and social divisions: for those who were baptized, the old divisions between Jew and Greek, slave and free, male and female had disappeared (Galatians 3:28). What this meant in practice is not altogether easy to see. It is evident that the old divisions still remained in society at large and that even within the church divisions based on gender and political status (slave and free) were not altogether set aside. What about the relations between Jew and Gentile? This was an issue over which Paul struggled. He wanted both to affirm the old covenant that God had made with his people the Jews (Romans 9:4) and also to insist that God was now calling the Gentiles. His own calling was to him the proof of this. Just as God was free to call the Jews in the first place, so too now he was not being inconsistent in calling the Gentiles.

## 4    The Temple

Members of the community at Qumran were opposed to the Temple hierarchy in Jerusalem. They had a different calendar and probably regarded the priests as polluted. By contrast they saw their own community and their own worship as in many ways a replacement for the Jerusalem Temple. Thus in 1QS 9:3-6 the community is said to constitute a 'house of holiness' and its worship and life is offered to 'atone for the fault of transgression and for the guilt of sin and for approval for the land, without the flesh of burnt offerings and without the fats of sacrifice.' The members looked forward on the other hand to a time when the Temple would be renewed and they would be restored as its rightful priests (11QTemple 29:8) (see above, pp.76-78).

Much of the New Testament is written in the aftermath of the destruction of the Temple and it is clear that the Temple does not feature seriously in its theologies. It is true that the first Christians in Jerusalem worshipped in the Temple, but this was a short-lived phase. John represents another kind of belief where worship is no longer centred on any particular place (John 4:20-24). What we find in the New Testament, particularly in Paul, is a similar tendency to refer to the community itself as the Temple of God (1 Corinthians 3:17; 6:19; 2 Corinthians 6:16).

## 5    Biblical interpretation

The literature of Qumran is shot through with biblical quotations, references and allusions - hardly surprising for a community which saw itself as living out a life in accordance with the Law and so much of whose energy was devoted to the production of Scripture and its understanding. One distinctive way in which Qumran uses Scripture is *pesher*, where a text such as Habakkuk is taken and commented on verse by verse in such a way as to illuminate the history of the community. The understanding behind this is clear: the prophets, though they were not aware of this, were in fact inspired to speak about the community. We also find *testimonia* - collections of biblical texts brought together to illuminate a particular theme (see above, pp.16-19).

Early Christian interpretation of the Bible is quite diverse. There is certainly nothing directly like the Habakkuk pesher, though in Romans 10:5-8 Paul does work his way through a passage from Deuteronomy 30:12-4. There is some evidence for the use of testimonia, most notably in the collection of sayings in Matthew which are introduced with the formula: 'this was to fulfill what the Lord had spoken by the prophet'. Here as also in 1 Peter 1:12 we have a conviction that the sayings of the prophets were intended to illuminate events in the life of the (Christian) community. But the use of Scripture is much wider than these technical uses. It provides the thought world which the New Testament writers draw on for their imagery, the theological concepts, and the 'grand narratives' which shape their writing about Jesus and their faith. Thus ideas like the restoration of God's glory to Mount Zion and the Gentiles' recognition of that glory (Isaiah 60; Ezekiel 34:30; 37:26-28) are taken up and reworked in Mark and Matthew's telling of the story of Jesus. When Jesus gathers the disciples together on the mountain in Galilee, declares to them that God has given him authority over all the earth, sends them out to make disciples of all nations, promising to be with them to the end of the age (Matthew 28:16-20), this passage is shot through with ideas and phrases from the biblical literature which treats of Zion.

6   Sin, flesh and dualism

One of the striking features of the Qumran literature is its dualistic language: light and darkness, truth and falsehood, wisdom and folly, righteousness and wickedness. The world is sharply divided; though as we have seen this division is ultimately rooted in God's decision to set two spirits over his world.

This dualism is both like and unlike that in the New Testament. Many scholars have seen a close connection between the language of John's Gospel and that of Qumran. The prologue of the gospel of John says: 'And the light shines in the darkness, and the darkness has not overcome it' (1:4). The Jews are told: 'You are of your father the devil, and your will is to do your father's desires. He was a murderer from the beginning, and has nothing to do with the truth, because there is no truth in him. When he lies, he speaks according to his own nature, for he is a liar and the father of lies' (John 8:44). However not all of the language works in quite the same way: John's Gospel makes a sharp contrast between flesh and spirit (as indeed does Paul): 'That which is born of flesh is flesh and that which is born of spirit is spirit' (John 3:6). While there is certainly a suggestion that John's opponents are in league with evil spirits, there is not the same interest in angelic powers as there is in Qumran. The believers are 'friends of Jesus' (15:12-17) rather than associates of angels (cf. the War Scroll with its vision of the men of the covenant fighting alongside the angels, 1QM 7:6).

Has there been any direct influence here? This is a fascinating but difficult question. Dualistic language of this kind is common enough in many religions. It can certainly be found in the Old Testament/Hebrew Bible and also in much contemporary Jewish literature (Jubilees, Testaments). Certainly the evidence of Qumran is impressive and has served to persuade many that the right milieu for the Gospel of John is a Jewish one. Nevertheless, this need not mean that there is any *direct* dependence of John on Qumran. What it does make clear is how much things in the Gospel are centred on Jesus as the Son. The role he plays is comparable in some ways to the Prince of Light in Qumran, ruling over the children of righteousness who walk in the ways of light (1QS 3:20). Jesus is the Good Shepherd (John 10:1-18) and will send his spirit to lead the disciples into all truth (16:13). But, equally, for other New Testament writers Jesus' role is closer to that of the Teacher of Righteousness. It is almost as if in Christian thought Jesus were assuming all the important roles, human and angelic, which, in first century Jewish thought, God uses to put the world to rights. The Qumran literature gives us wonderfully rich evidence of this kind of thought. It does not necessarily gives us the direct source of the images and concepts which the New Testament writers used to express their particular beliefs.

# 6    FURTHER READING

Translations of Dead Sea Scrolls

Florentino García Martínez
  *The Dead Sea Scrolls Translated* (2nd Edition, E J Brill, 1996)
Geza Vermes
  *The Dead Sea Scrolls in English* (Revised and Extended 4th
    Edition, Penguin, 1995)
Michael Wise, Martin Abegg Jr. and Edward Cook
  *The Dead Sea Scrolls: a New Translation* (HarperCollins,
    1996)

Introductions to the Dead Sea Scrolls/Qumran

Klaus Berger
  *Jesus and the Dead Sea Scrolls:  The Truth Under Lock and
    Key?* (Westminster/John Knox Press, 1995)
Otto Betz and Rainer Riesner
  *Jesus, Qumran and the Vatican* (SCM Press, 1994)
Jonathan Campbell
  *Deciphering the Dead Sea Scrolls* (Fontana Press, 1996)

James Charlesworth (editor)

*Jesus and the Dead Sea Scrolls* (Doubleday 1992)

John J Collins

*The Scepter and the Star: The Messiahs of the Dead Sea
Scrolls and Other Ancient Literature* (Doubleday 1995)

Philip R Davies

*Qumran* (Guildford, 1982)

Philip R Davies

*Behind the Essenes: History and Ideology in the Dead Sea
Scrolls* (Scholars Press, 1987)

Robert Eisenman and Michael Wise

*The Dead Sea Scrolls Uncovered: The First Complete
Translation and Interpretation of 50 Key Documents
Withheld for Over 35 Years* (Element, 1992)

Joseph A Fitzmyer

*Responses to 101 Questions on the Dead Sea Scrolls* (G
Chapman, 1992)

Norman Golb

*Who Wrote the Dead Sea Scrolls? The Search for the Secret of
Qumran* (Scribner, 1995)

Michael A Knibb

*The Qumran Community* (Cambridge University Press, 1987)

Florentino García Martínez and J L Barrera

*The People of the Dead Sea Scrolls* (E J Brill, 1995)

Lawrence Schiffman

*Reclaiming the Dead Sea Scrolls* (Doubleday, 1994)

Hershel Shanks (editor)

*Understanding the Dead Sea Scrolls* (SPCK, 1992)

James C VanderKam

*The Dead Sea Scrolls Today* (SPCK 1994)

Geza Vermes

*The Dead Sea Scrolls: Qumran in Perspective* (HarperCollins, 1994)


## General Books on Early Judaism

Shaye J D Cohen

*From the Maccabees to the Mishnah* (SPCK, 1987)

Martin Jafee

*Early Judaism* (Prentice Hall, 1997)

A R C Leaney

*The Jewish and Christian World, 200 BC to AD 200* (Cambridge University Press, 1984)

Doron Mendels

*The Rise and Fall of Jewish Nationalism* (Doubleday, 1992)

E P Sanders

*Judaism: Practice and Belief 63 BCE-66CE* (SCM, 1990)

Yigael Yadin

*Masada: Herod's Fortress and the Zealots' Last Stand* (Phoenix Illustrated, 1997)


## General Books on Jesus and Early Christianity

John Barclay and John Sweet (editors)

*Early Christian Thought in its Jewish Context* (Cambridge University Press, 1996)

Marcus Borg

*Jesus in Contemporary Scholarship* (Trinity Press International, 1994)

J Dominic Crossan

*The Historical Jesus: The Life of a Mediterranean Jewish Peasant* (T & T Clark, 1991)

Bart D Ehrman

*The New Testament. A Historical Introduction to the Early Christian Writings* (Oxford University Press, 1997)

John Riches

*The World of Jesus* (Cambridge University Press, 1990)

E P Sanders

*The Historical Figure of Jesus* (Penguin, 1993)

Graham Stanton

*The Gospels and Jesus* (Oxford University Press, 1989)

Graham Stanton

*Gospel Truth? New Light on Jesus and the Gospels* (HarperCollins, 1995)

Geza Vermes

*Jesus the Jew* (SCM, 1983)

Geza Vermes

*The Religion of Jesus the Jew* (SCM, 1993)

N T Wright

*Jesus and the Victory of God* (SPCK, 1996)

# GLOSSARY OF TERMS

**apocalyptic**

used in the first instance of literature, in which divine secrets are revealed. Since these often concern the course of history, including the future, the term is used by extension for vivid expectations of 'the end', usually characterised by sharp antitheses between 'this world' and 'the world to come', and between 'the elect' and 'the unrighteous'.

**apocrypha**

a body of Jewish texts which were included in the Septuagint but not in the Hebrew Bible.

**Apocryphon**

a rewritten version of a biblical story, with many additions, as in the Genesis Apocryphon.

**canon**

an authoritative body of texts, regarded in some sense as a unified 'Scripture'.

**covenant**

a contract relationship between the elect and God.

**eschatology/eschatological**

talk and study of 'the last things'; by extension, anything relating to the 'endtime'. In Qumran it is partly 'realized', i.e. the endtime conditions are partially present already.

**Essenes**

a movement within Judaism with a distinctive discipline of life: see Section Three.

**exegesis/exegetical**

explanation and interpretation of a text.

**florilegium**

collection of biblical verses on a common theme.

## halakhah/halakhic

from the Hebrew term 'to walk': laws which define the pattern of life in its practical details.

## Hasmonean

the dynasty deriving from the Maccabean family; the period of their rule: see Chronology.

## Hellenization

cultural adaptation to the Greek tradition (political, social, economic, ideological etc.)

## Herodian

the dynasty of Herod the Great and his sons; the period of their rule: see Chronology.

## Josephus

Jewish historian (37-c.100 CE) who provides our only full account of Judaean history and of its various parties, including the Essenes. His works include his *Life*, *The Jewish War* and *Jewish Antiquities*.

## lustrations

washing, bathing etc.

## Maccabees

the family which led the uprising against the Hellenization of Judaea: see Chronology.

## Masoretic Text (MT)

the text of the Hebrew Bible fixed in its definitive form between 600 and 900 CE.

## messianic

hopes and movements focusing on one or more Messiahs (figures anointed by God for decisive action in the endtime).

## midrash

commentary on a text, often employing further texts or legendary material.

## Mishnah

the first published collection (c.200 CE) in organised form of the various halakhic laws of rabbinic Judaism.

## palaeography

the study of ancient handwriting, often with a view to its dating.

## pesher/pesharim

a Qumran term for 'interpretation' or 'solution', giving rise to a distinctive verse-by-verse pattern of commentary.

## Pharisees

movement within Second Temple Judaism characterised by exact and generally humane interpretation of the Law; was to survive the destruction of the Temple and give birth to rabbinic Judaism.

## Philo

Jewish philosopher from Alexandria (c.20 BCE - 50 CE), who wrote idealised accounts of the Essenes' lifestyle.

## Pliny the Elder

Roman aristocrat and traveller (23-79 CE) who included a short notice on the Essenes in his *Natural History*.

## rabbinic Judaism

the form of Judaism which took shape after the destruction of the Temple (70 CE) and reached its first stage of definition in the publication of the Mishnah (200 CE).

## Sadducees

in a broad sense, a priestly party (sons of Zadok); the term is used by Josephus and the New Testament to refer to a party of aristocratic and Hellenizing priests, who were inclined to compromise with the Romans.

## Samaritans

inhabitants of Samaria whose political and cultural history rendered them inferior in the eyes of Judaean Jews, but who considered themselves proper 'sons of Israel'; they did not recognise the legitimacy of the Jerusalem Temple.

**Second Temple**

the Jerusalem Temple constructed after the return from exile and enlarged by Herod; see Chronology.

**sect/sectarian**

a group which breaks away from its parent body but claims more or less exclusive rights to the status of that body; a sectarian outlook is one focused on the narrow horizons of the sect, with the conviction that others' viewpoints are incorrect.

**Seleucid**

see Chronology.

**Septuagint**

Greek translation of the Hebrew Bible, begun in Alexandria in the third century BCE.

**Targum**

Aramaic paraphrase of the Hebrew Bible.

**testimonia**

collection of biblical passages on a common theme.

**Testament**

a literary genre, comprising a death-bed scene of a famous figure giving his final instructions.

**Torah**

textually defined, the five books of Moses (the Pentateuch) forming the first part of the Hebrew Bible; the others are the Prophets and the Writings. Torah also means 'Law', though with a broader sense than our English term, and more akin to 'Teaching' or 'Revelation'.

**Wadi**

a ravine down which flash floods stream into a valley. Wadi Qumran is the ravine next to the Qumran ruins which provided water for the settlement.